WITHDRAWN

UK Publisher: Sally Smith
Production Manager: Daniel Mersey
Commissioning Editor: Fiona Quinn
Development Editor: Joe Fullman
Content Editor: Erica Peters
Photo Research: Jill Emeny
Cartography: Jeremy Norton

Wiley also publishes its books in a variety of electronic formats. Some
content that appears in print may not be available in electronic books.

British Library Cataloguing in Publication Data

A catalogue record for this book is available from the British Library

ISBN: 978-0-470-79422-7 (pbk), ISBN: 978-0-470-97467-4 (ebk)

Typeset by Wiley Indianapolis Composition Services

Printed and bound in China by RR Donnelley

5 4 3 2 1

A Note from the Editorial Director

Organizing your time. That's what this guide is all about.

Other guides give you long lists of things to see and do and then expect you to fit the pieces together. The Day by Day guides are different. These guides tell you the best of everything, and then they show you how to see it *in the smartest, most time-efficient way*. Our authors have designed detailed itineraries organized by time, neighborhood, or special interest. And each tour comes with a bulleted map that takes you from stop to stop.

Hoping to stroll the streets admiring the Art Nouveau architecture, enjoy a beer or two, or savour Belgian chocolates? Planning a rummage at the flea market or plotting a day of funfilled activities with the kids? Whatever your interest or schedule, the Day by Days give you the smartest routes to follow. Not only do we take you to the top attractions, hotels, and restaurants, but we also help you access those special moments that locals get to experience— those "finds" that turn tourists into travelers.

The Day by Days are also your top choice if you're looking for one complete guide for all your travel needs. The best hotels and restaurants for every budget, the greatest shopping values, the wildest nightlife—it's all here.

Why should you trust our judgment? Because our authors personally visit each place they write about. They're an independent lot who say what they think and would never include places they wouldn't recommend to their best friends. They're also open to suggestions from readers. If you'd like to contact them, please send your comments our way at feedback@frommers.com, and we'll pass them on.

Enjoy your Day by Day guide—the most helpful travel companion you can buy. And have the trip of a lifetime.

Warm regards,

Kelly Regan WITHDRAWN

Kelly Regan, Editorial Director

Frommer's Travel Guides

About the Author

After co-writing books on Japanese prints and on guitars, **Mary Anne Evans** turned to her more immediate surroundings and became one of the leading travel writers on London and Britain, specializing in restaurants and hotels. Several guidebooks and many magazine articles later, Europe beckoned, particularly Belgium, a country which is still one of Europe's lesser-known gems.

Acknowledgments

My special thanks to development editor Donald Strachan, to Sophie Bouchard in Brussels, and Anne de Meerleer in Bruges for all their sound advice and help and to Ossi Laurila for his great photographs. And finally to my good friend, Ann Janssen, for accompanying me on long walks through Brussels and for the use of her spare room.

An Additional Note

Please be advised that travel information is subject to change at any time—and this is especially true of prices. We therefore suggest that you write or call ahead for confirmation when making your travel plans. The authors, editors, and publisher cannot be held responsible for the experiences of readers while traveling. Your safety is important to us, however, so we encourage you to stay alert and be aware of your surroundings.

Star Ratings, Icons & Abbreviations

Every hotel, restaurant, and attraction listing in this guide has been ranked for quality, value, service, amenities, and special features using a **star-rating system.** Hotels, restaurants, attractions, shopping, and nightlife are rated on a scale of zero stars (recommended) to three stars (exceptional). In addition to the star-rating system, we also use a **kids icon** to point out the best bets for families. Within each tour, we recommend cafes, bars, or restaurants where you can take a break. Each of these stops appears in a shaded box marked with a coffee-cup-shaped bullet ☕.

The following **abbreviations** are used for credit cards:

AE	American Express	DISC	Discover	V	Visa
DC	Diners Club	MC	MasterCard		

Travel Resources at Frommers.com

Frommer's travel resources don't end with this guide. Frommer's website, **www.frommers.com**, has travel information on more than 4,000 destinations. We update features regularly, giving you access to the most current trip-planning information and the best airfare, lodging, and car-rental bargains. You can also listen to podcasts, connect with other Frommers.com members through our active-reader forums, share your travel photos, read blogs from guidebook editors and fellow travelers, and much more.

A Note on Prices

In the "Take a Break" and "Best Bets" sections of this book, we have used a system of dollar signs to show a range of costs for 1 night in a hotel (the price of a double-occupancy room) or the cost of an entree (main course) at a restaurant. Use the following table to decipher the dollar signs:

Cost	Hotels	Restaurants
$	under $100	under $10
$$	$100–$200	$10–$20
$$$	$200–$300	$20–$30
$$$$	$300–$400	$30–$40
$$$$$	over $400	over $40

How to Contact Us

In researching this book, we discovered many wonderful places—hotels, restaurants, shops, and more. We're sure you'll find others. Please tell us about them, so we can share the information with your fellow travelers in upcoming editions. If you were disappointed with a recommendation, we'd love to know that, too. Please write to:

Frommer's Brussels & Bruges Day by Day, 2nd Edition
Wiley Publishing, Inc. • 111 River St. • Hoboken, NJ 07030-577

WITHDRAWN

12 Favorite
Moments

12 Favorite **Moments** in Brussels

1. Grand' Place
2. Musée des Beaux-Arts
3. A la Mort Subite
4. Jeu de Balle flea market
5. Art Nouveau
6. Cartoon trails
7. Viva M'Boma
8. L'Archiduc

Bruges

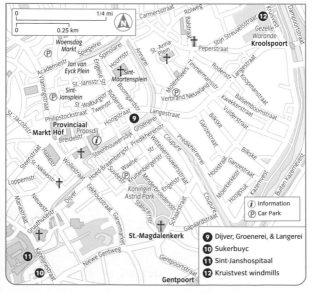

i Information
P Car Park

9. Dijver, Groenerei, & Langerei
10. Sukerbuyc
11. Sint-Janshospitaal
12. Kruisvest windmills

Discovering cartoon murals in a narrow side-street, drinking in a bar once frequented by singer Jacques Brel, marveling at Flemish Old Masters, admiring the curves of an Art Nouveau balcony—these are just a few of the glories of Brussels, a city that rewards and surprises first-time visitors. And although Bruges is well trodden, it possesses such riches that you'll always discover something new.

The glorious Grand' Place.

❶ **Walking through the Grand' Place** as the morning starts and the crowds have not yet appeared. I can stand in the middle of this glorious medieval and baroque square, look up at the skyline of gabled houses and pitched roofs, and imagine what it was like to live in this bustling, prosperous city 400 years ago. *See p 8.*

❷ **Standing in front of *The Census at Bethlehem*** by Pieter Brueghel the Elder in the Musée des Beaux-Arts. Take in the small details of 16th-century Flemish life: chickens scratch for food in the

Chapter opener page: The Grand' Place, Brussels.

snow, figures skate on the frozen river, a child pulls his fractious companion along. It's an artwork of breathtaking observation. *See p 63.*

❸ **Downing a glass of 'Sudden Death' beer in A la Mort Subite** and waiting for that Jacques Brel moment to come, when I start humming '*Le Plat Pays*.' Jacques Brel's favorite local is still full of Belgian beer fans. *See p 115.*

❹ **Trying to pick up a bargain at the Jeu de Balle flea market** on Sunday morning, and then joining the smart Bruxellois wandering and window-shopping in Rue Haute and Rue Blaes. *See p 71.*

❺ **Exploring Brussels' Art Nouveau heritage.** Whichever route I roam, I always find myself discovering

The Sunday morning Jeu de Balle market.

A windmill marks the outer ramparts of Bruges.

new streets full of gems by late 19th- and early 20th-century architects— they created the greatest Art Nouveau city in Europe. *See p 32.*

6 Coming across one of the many giant cartoons painted on the side of a perfectly ordinary house. Blown up so large, the surreal touches and stylistic excesses from the original comics make a real impact. *See p 49.*

7 Tucking into a hearty plate of *stoemp* (mashed potato with root vegetables, cream, bacon, and spices) at Viva M'Boma after a day in one of Brussels' major museums. Belgians have their mix of high art and life's basic comforts just right. *See p 108.*

8 Listening to a jazz legend in L'Archiduc and talking music with the folks at the next table. Brussels is a friendly city and people are more than happy to chat, particularly if you have shared interests. *See p 126.*

9 Discovering that Bruges really is the Venice of the North. Walk along any of the canalside roads, such as the Dijver, Groenerei, or Langerei, early in the morning when nobody's up yet, or at night when the brick buildings are lit up. You

get a sense of the importance of the waterways to this medieval trading city. *See p 142.*

10 Buying chocolate from any of Bruges' artisan chocolatiers. My favorite is Sukerbuyc, where the smell of chocolate bubbling away at the back of the shop always gets my taste buds going. After a major buying spree, I cross the road for a cup of hot chocolate at De Proverie. It's like a solemn Japanese tea ceremony, Bruges style. *See p 151.*

11 Admiring Hans Memling's St.-Ursula Shrine in the Sint-Janshospitaal. This painted reliquary, shaped like a traditional house complete with steep roof, is one of Belgium's great works of art. In this darkened medieval building, the mix of the brutal and the sublime that was medieval Belgium comes alive. *See p 143.*

12 Renting a bicycle and riding out east of the center. Quiet streets bring you to four windmills that mark the outer ramparts of Bruges. Toward the west, gaze over the rooftops of the city; to the east lie the flat polders of this part of Belgium. Locals come here at weekends to walk their dogs and picnic with their children. *See p 145.* ●

The Best **in One Day**

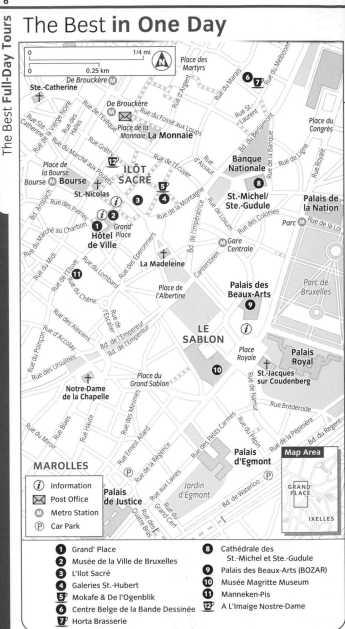

0 | 1/4 mi
0 | 0.25 km

Place des Martyrs

De Brouckère Ⓜ

✝ Ste.-Catherine

De Brouckère Ⓜ

✉ Place de la Monnaie **La Monnaie**

Rue du Marais **6** **7**

Rue St. Laurent

Rue du Berlaimont

Place du Congrès

Place de la Bourse **Bourse** Ⓜ

Bourse

12

✝ **St.-Nicolas**

Ⓘ

Ⓘ **ILÔT SACRÉ**

5

3 **4**

Banque Nationale

8

Rue de la Banque

Rue Royale

1

Hôtel de Ville

Grand' Place

St.-Michel/ Ste.-Gudule

Rue des Colonies

Palais de la Nation

Ⓜ **Parc**

Rue de la Loi

✝ **La Madeleine**

Place de l'Albertine

Ⓜ **Gare Centrale**

Palais des Beaux-Arts

9

Parc de Bruxelles

11

Place de l'Albertine

ⓘ

LE SABLON

Place Royale

✝ **St.-Jacques sur Coudenberg**

Palais Royal

✝ **Notre-Dame de la Chapelle**

Place du Grand Sablon

10

Rue de Namur

Rue Bréderode

Bd. du Régent

MAROLLES

Ⓟ

Palais d'Egmont

Ⓟ

Map Area

GRAND' PLACE

ⓘ Information
✉ Post Office
Ⓜ Metro Station
Ⓟ Car Park

Palais de Justice

Jardin d'Egmont

Bd. de Waterloo

IXELLES

1 Grand' Place
2 Musée de la Ville de Bruxelles
3 L'Ilot Sacré
4 Galeries St.-Hubert
5 Mokafe & De l'Ogenblik
6 Centre Belge de la Bande Dessinée
7 Horta Brasserie
8 Cathédrale des St.-Michel et Ste.-Gudule
9 Palais des Beaux-Arts (BOZAR)
10 Musée Magritte Museum
11 Manneken-Pis
12 A L'Imaige Nostre-Dame

Previous page: Notre-Dame-du-Sablon.

Brussels is not just about the Grand' Place and the huge buildings of the European Parliament; it's also full of surprises. I recommend you get a feel of the city through its own mix of the sacred and the profane: the best of its art and local history, a taste of Art Nouveau, comics, elegant shopping, and of course, beer.
START: Métro to Bourse.

The Grand' Place.

1 ★★★ **Grand' Place.** It never palls. Every time I emerge from one of the crowded, cobbled, medieval streets into the Grand' Place, I marvel at this perfect Flemish Renaissance square. Even the crowds of tourists can't destroy the feeling that I've stepped into an Old Master painting. Lined by its guild houses and Hôtel de Ville, the Grand' Place was the administrative heart of a city made prosperous by 17th-century commerce. *See minitour p 8.*

2 ★ **kids Musée de la Ville de Bruxelles.** I'm always surprised that the Museum of Brussels isn't busier. Housed in the **Maison du Roi** (King's House), a late 19th-century reconstruction of Charles V's original 1515 building, it's an easily digestible mix of objects, from tapestries to silver and gold, illustrating

the city's history. Large-scale models and pictures on the next floor build an image of old Brussels. Children should make for the top floor and the extensive wardrobe of the Manneken-Pis statue (**11**). More than 650 national costumes from around the world have been donated by misguided visiting heads of state. ⏱ *45 min. Maison du Roi, Grand' Place.* ☎ *02 279 43 50. www.brucity.be. Admission 3€ adults, 1.50€ children. Tues–Sun 10am–5pm. Closed public holidays. Métro: Bourse.*

3 **L'Ilot Sacré.** Walk out of the square on the northeast side into L'Ilot Sacré (the Sacred Island), a maze of narrow medieval streets that are as crowded today as they were when the **Rue du Marché aux Herbes** and **Rue de la**

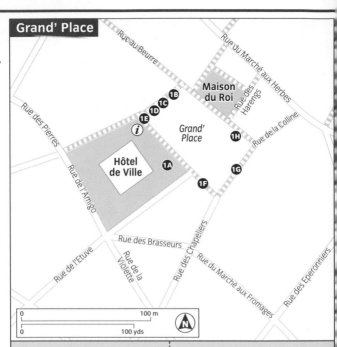

Grand' Place

To get the full wow factor, stand in the middle of the Grand' Place with Brussels' town hall, the **1A Hôtel de Ville,** to your left. Guided tours take in its elegant official rooms; for the full Gothic effect, you can get married here if one of you is a Belgian resident. Many of the old guild houses were named after the first buildings on the site, not the guilds (trade associations) that later occupied them. Nos. 1–2, **1B** the grand **Maison des Boulangers** (Baker's House) with a gold head of St. Lambert, patron saint of bakers, was purpose-built as the guild house; today it contains the Roy d'Espagne bar/restaurant. No. 3, **1C La Brouette** (note 'The Wheelbarrow' over the door) belonged to the tallow (candle) merchants; no. 4, **1D Le Sac** (The Sack) to the cabinetmakers and coopers; no. 6, **1E Le Cornet** (The Horn), covered in marine symbols, was the boatmen's guild house. No. 9, **1F Le Cygne** (The Swan) became the butcher's guild house in 1720. The revolutionary 19th-century philosophers Karl Marx and Friedrich Engels drank in a bar in what is now an expensive restaurant, **La Maison du Cygne**. The single facade of **1G Nos. 13–19** is decorated with the busts of 19 dukes of Brabant, the eldest sons of the ruler and traditional heirs to the throne; the tailors occupied nos. 24–25 before it became **1H La Chaloupe d'Or** bar/restaurant. ⏲ *30 min. Hôtel de Ville guided tours Tues & Wed 3:15pm; 3€ adults; 1.50€ children 6–15 ; free for children 5 and under.*

Musée de la Ville de Bruxelles.

Montagne were staging posts on the lucrative trade route between Bruges and Cologne. The **Rue des Bouchers** is lined with restaurants, serving fish as well as the meat that gave the street its name, 'Butchers' Street.' ⏱ *15 min.*

❹ ★★ **Shopping in the Galeries St.-Hubert.** Just north of the Grand' Place, three glass-vaulted galleries—the **Galerie de la Reine** (Queen's), **Galerie du Roi** (King's), and **Galerie des Princes** (Princes')— make up the mid-19th-century Galeries St.-Hubert. I love the mixture of people here: serious readers make for venerable **Tropismes**, 11 galerie des Princes (☎ 02 512 88 52; www.tropismes.be) for its range of books in French; chocoholics' dreams are answered at **Corné Port-Royal**, 5 galerie de la Reine (☎ 02 213 62 22; www.corne-port-royal.be) or **Neuhaus**, 25–27 galerie de la Reine (☎ 02 512 63 59; www.neuhaus.be); those after genuine quality lace go to **Manufacture Belge de Dentelles,** 6–8 galerie de la Reine (☎ 02 511 44 77; www.mbd.be); while the accessory-challenged are buying expensive handbags in **Delvaux,** 31 galerie de la Reine (☎ 02 512 71 98; www.delvaux.be). ⏱ *1 hr. Rue du Marché aux Herbes. Métro: Gare Centrale.*

☕ **5** ★ I always recover from a retail assault with a coffee at **Mokafe,** 9 galerie du Roi (☎ 02 511 78 70; $); or opt for a seasonal dish from the daily menu at **De l'Ogenblik,** 1 galerie des Princes (☎ 02 511 61 51; $$).

❻ ★★ **kids Centre Belge de la Bande Dessinée.** It's appropriate that the country of Tintin opened Europe's first museum devoted to the ninth art—the comic strip (*bande dessinée*). It's housed in the former

Hôtel de Ville.

The glass-vaulted Galeries St.-Hubert.

Waucquez warehouse, a wholesale draper's built by Victor Horta in 1906 in the Art Nouveau style. Inside, Tintin, Snowy and Captain Haddock, Spirou, Gaston Lagaffe, the Smurfs, Lucky Luke, and countless other famous names from Belgian comics illustrate the genre's history. Odd room settings are irresistible to photographers. Changing exhibitions also dip in and out of the museum's vast collections. ⏱ *1 hr. 20 rue des Sables.* ☎ *02 219 19 80. www.comics center.net. Admission 7.50€ adults, 6€ children 12–18, free for children 11 and under. Tues–Sun 10am–6pm. Métro: Botanique or Parc.*

7 ★ kids **Horta Brasserie.** The bar here is often frequented by parents waiting for children who can't be prised away from Tintin. The menu runs from Belgian classics to pasta and meatballs, though I've yet to spot a tourist ordering the horse stew, just like grandma used to cook. *20 rue des Sables.* ☎ *02 217 72 71. www.brasseriehorta.be. $$.*

8 ★★ **Cathédrale des St.-Michel et Ste.-Gudule.** Modeled on Notre Dame in Paris, the mainly 16th-century French Gothic church overlooks the town—although any grandeur is spoiled by surrounding office buildings. Members of the Belgian royal family are married and crowned here (though not buried: that privilege belongs to Notre-Dame de Laeken, p 74, **1**. Protestants in 1579 and then, in 1793, the invading French Republican Army, stripped the interior of its treasures, but look for the 16th-century stained glass windows where religion is tempered by secular power in the form of Emperor Charles V and his family. Try to catch Sunday mass at 10am for Gregorian chant by the cathedral singers. ⏱ *45 min. Parvis Sainte-Gudule.* ☎ *02 217 83 45. www.cathedralestmichel.be. Free admission. Mon–Fri 7am–7pm (Winter to 6pm), Sat 9:30am–3:30pm; Sun 2–6pm. Treasury 1€: Mon–Fri 10am–12:30pm & 2–5pm; Sat 10am–12:30pm & 2–3pm; Sun 2–5pm. Métro: Gare Centrale.*

9 ★★ **Palais des Beaux-Arts (BOZAR).** Designed by architect Victor Horta (1861–1947) in, rather

Entrance to the Palais des Beaux-Arts.

The Musée Magritte Museum is housed in a neoclassical 19th-century building.

surprisingly for him, Art Deco style, and finished in 1928, this is one of the most dynamic of Brussels' arts centers, staging cutting-edge exhibitions from national and international artists, as well as classical music concerts and performances. *See p 125.*

⑩ ★★★ **Musée Magritte Museum.** Devoted to surrealist painter, René Magritte, the museum opened in June 2009. It brings the first half of the 20th century and the artist himself dramatically to life through films, graphic art, photographs, and paintings. It contains the richest collection of Magritte's work in the world with more than 200 examples, and is one of Brussels' biggest attractions. Buy tickets online to avoid the queues. *See p 59,* ❸.

⑪ kids **Manneken-Pis.** Make your way down through the gardens of the Mont des Arts to Rue St.-Jean. Galerie Bortier is a rather dusty 19th-century arcade of shops selling secondhand books and prints. From Rue Lombard, turn left into Rue de l'Etuve for two classic city sights: to your right, a cartoon painted on the side of a house shows Tintin, Captain Haddock, and Snowy escaping from their hotel via the fire escape; to your left, hordes gawp at Manneken Pis, the bronze statue of a small boy peeing merrily away which has, bizarrely, become the symbol of Brussels. ⏱ *20 min. Métro: Bourse.*

⑫ ★ **A L'Imaige de Nostre-Dame.** If you've restrained yourselves all day, it's time to try a glass—or several—of Belgium's famous golden nectar. Tucked away in a cul-de-sac off Rue du Marché aux Herbes, this two-room space has wooden tables, friendly staff, and even a Dutch dresser. And its beer range is legendary. *Impasse des Cadeaux.* ☎ *02 219 42 49.* $.

Manneken-Pis is Brussels' best-known character.

The Best **in Two Days**

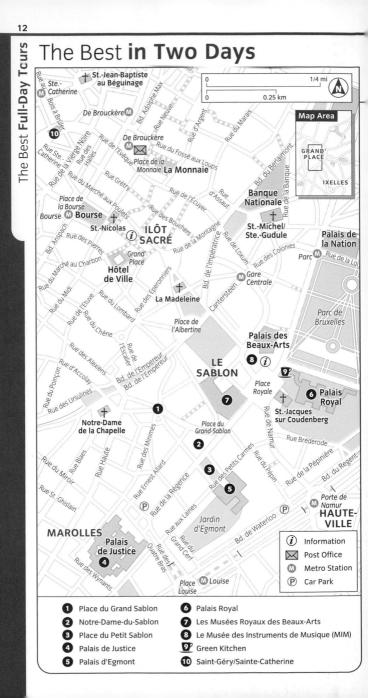

1 Place du Grand Sablon	**6** Palais Royal	
2 Notre-Dame-du-Sablon	**7** Les Musées Royaux des Beaux-Arts	
3 Place du Petit Sablon	**8** Le Musée des Instruments de Musique (MIM)	
4 Palais de Justice	**9** Green Kitchen	
5 Palais d'Egmont	**10** Saint-Géry/Sainte-Catherine	

Start with my favorite Brussels' pastime of people-watching from a pavement cafe, and then go from posh, conservative Brussels to the newly fashionable areas west of the Grand' Place, where Brussels was born. START: **Tram 92, 94 to Petit Sablon.**

1 ★ Place du Grand Sablon.
A great place to start the day, where high-end Brussels congregates and wealthy ladies rub shoulders with antique dealers taking a break from their shops lining the 17th-century square. There's also a good weekend **antiques market** (Sat 9am–6pm, Sun 9am–2pm). The smell of freshly baked bread entices you into the bakery/deli, **Le Pain Quotidien**, 11 rue des Sablons (☎ 02 513 51 54; $), past the wooden shop counter to the conservatory at the back. **Wittamer,** 13 place du Grand-Sablon (☎ 02 546 11 11; $) is a real Brussels institution: Try the hot chocolate in the cafe at this venerable pâtisserie. ⏱ *1 hr. Bus: 95 to Grand Sablon.*

2 ★ Notre-Dame-du-Sablon.
Religion and fashion have always gone hand in hand, and so when

Place du Grand Sablon.

Margaret of Austria (Emperor Charles V's Regent) joined the cult of the Madonna, whose statue was believed to have arrived here by divine intervention, the wealthy followed and the church was rebuilt in the 15th century as Notre-Dame. The flamboyant Flemish edifice has two baroque chapels—built for the Turn and Taxis family whose wealth came from setting up the first public postal system in Europe in 1516— tombs of other wealthy families, and richly colored stained-glass windows, though its altarpieces are now in the Musees Royaux des Beaux-Arts (p 14, **7**; p 62) and Maison du Roi (p 7, **2**). ⏱ *20 min. 38 rue de la Régence.* ☎ *02 511 57 41. Free admission. Mon–Fri 9am– 6:30pm; Sat & Sun 10am–7pm. Tram: 92, 94 to Petit Sablon.*

3 ★ Place du Petit Sablon. I love the sense of peace and history (and the shade on a sweltering day) of these small formal gardens, laid out in 1890. Statues of the dashing Counts of Egmont and Hoorn, executed in 1568 for joining a rebellion against the savage rule of King Philip II, dominate a large fountain while 48 small statues representing Brussels' medieval guilds surround the gardens. ⏱ *15 min. Place du Petit Sablon, Rue de la Régence. Tram: 92, 94 to Petit Sablon.*

4 Palais de Justice. This monstrous carbuncle of a building dominates its surroundings. Conceived by King Léopold I in 1833, it was left to his son, the megalomaniac Léopold II, to build it. The interior is equally formidable, striking terror into guilty and innocent alike. From nearby place Poelaert, there are

Place du Petit Sablon.

views of the city's church towers, turrets, and in the distance, the Atomium (p 53, **9**). ⏱ *20 min. See p 23, **2**.*

5 **Palais d'Egmont.** This palace, built in 1534 for the mother of the executed count of Egmont (**3**), was rebuilt in the 1890s and now houses Belgium's **Ministry of Foreign Affairs.** Britain, Ireland, and Denmark signed the treaty admitting them to the European Economic Community (now the European Union) here in 1972. ⏱ *10 min.*

6 ★ **Palais Royal.** This rather squat palace isn't favored by the current royal family, who prefer the Chateau Royal (p 75, **4**) in leafy Laeken. The Palais' gilded formal rooms, full of overstuffed furniture, are open to the public when the royals are on summer vacation; don't miss the tapestries in the Goya salon and some over-the-top chandeliers in the Throne Room. External photographs are best left until after dark, when the building is floodlit. ⏱ *30 min. 1000 place des Palais.* ☎ *02 551 20 20. www.monarchie.be. Free admission. July–Sept, Tues–Sun 10:30am–5pm. Métro: Trône. Tram: 92, 94 to Royale.*

7 ★★★ **Les Musées Royaux des Beaux-Arts.** This blockbuster of a museum is divided into the **Musée d'Art Ancien** (15th–18th century), the **Musée d'Art Moderne** (19th century onward), and the new **Musée Magritte Museum** (p 59, **3**). It's huge, and so pick and choose, something I find almost impossible when faced with Flemish primitives. Then there's the extraordinary journey through the Symbolists, surrealists, and an eye-opening collection of native artists in the Modern Art Museum. *See Special Interest Tours, p 62.*

8 ★★★ kids **Le Musée des Instruments de Musique (MIM).** What do you do with an old department store? The Belgians turned this 1899 Art Nouveau building (formerly the **Old England** department store) into the hugely popular Musical Instruments Museum. It now displays hundreds of instruments from its collection of some 7,000, the biggest in the world. Don your headphones, approach the displays, and music played on the

Le Musée des Instruments de Musique in the Old England Building.

Brussels in Europe

Brussels is home to the European Union's main institutions, and Members of the European Parliament (MEPs) also have their offices here. Building the institutions to house this massive bureaucracy began in the 1960s; today the huge glass and steel buildings dominate the 'European district,' a relatively small area, which empties one week a month when sessions are held in Strasbourg, the official seat. The Union is currently made up of 27 countries, with another three official candidates waiting in the wings, making up a whopping 500 million citizens. Already the second largest democracy in the world (after India), the Union is growing hugely, making Brussels a vastly important city. But surprisingly, and delightfully, when you're in the center of Brussels, it feels like the small capital city that it is, and not the center of Europe.

instruments you're looking at pipes up. Walk from booming Tibetan temple trumpets to tinkling clavichords; hear the medieval Cornemuse, depicted in paintings by Pieter Brueghel the Younger, and glaze over at the purity of a 16th-century flute. Don't miss the prototype of the saxophone, invented by the Belgian Adolphe Sax. ⏱ *1½ hr. 2 rue Montagne de la Cour.* ☎ *02 545 01 30. www.mim. be. Admission 5€ adults (extra for exhibitions), free 1st Wed of the month from 1pm, and for children 11 and under. Tues–Fri 9:30am–4:45pm, Sat & Sun 10am–4:45pm. Closed public holidays. Métro: Porte de Namur or Gare Centrale. Tram: 92, 94 to Royale.*

9 ★ kids **Green Kitchen.** The emphasis is on freshness and healthy eating, and so tuck into delicious salads, soups, and sandwiches, straight from farmer Paulux's fields. The summertime courtyard is a real bonus as is the great weekend brunch. The restaurant is part of the BELvue Museum—well worth a quiet hour's visit. ☎ *02 545 08 09. www. green-kitchen.be. $.*

10 ★★ **Saint-Géry/Sainte-Catherine.** From the museum, walk to the Grand' Place, over the Boulevard Anspach, and into Place St.-Géry (15 min), or catch the no. 95 bus to Bourse and walk from there. Legend has it that Place St.-Géry is the birthplace of Brussels, which expanded from a 6th-century chapel here into the medieval town. In more recent years, St.-Géry has been reborn as the latest hip and happening area, with clusters of bars in which to hang out. The surrounding streets and Rue Antoine Dansaert have attracted so many fashion designers that Brussels now challenges Antwerp as Belgium's premier design city. To the north, Place Sainte-Catherine was the heart of the original working port and fish market. The river was paved over, but the area retains a quayside feeling; it's the place for restaurants serving the freshest fish, best washed down with chilled Moselle wine. ⏱ *2 hr. See p 66. Avoid Sun and Mon when the fish is less flappingly fresh and many shops and restaurants are closed.*

The Best **in Three Days**

1. Parlement Européen
2. Musée Wiertz
3. Muséum des Sciences Naturelles
4. Parc Léopold
5. Maison Antoine
6. European Union buildings
7. Walking the Art Nouveau route
8. Casa Italiana
9. Parc du Cinquantenaire
10. Maison de Paul Cauchie
11. Aux Délices de Capoue

Love it or hate it, the Quartier Européen is as much a part of the capital as the Grand' Place. Wandering around makes a good start to a day that also takes in older grand designs of Léopold II, plus the Art Nouveau delights of Square Ambiorix. Wear stout shoes, and kick off in one of the little cafes lining the Place du Luxembourg. **START: Bus no. 95 to Place du Luxembourg.**

1 ★ **Parlement Européen.** A walkway through the station at the end of Place du Luxembourg takes you through the main European Parliament building, housing the various committees (debates take place in Strasbourg, France). The workings of the European Union are so labyrinthine that it's not worth trying to figure them out; just take the short audio guide tour to glimpse the beast housed inside. The building is known locally as the 'Caprice of the Gods'—both a reference to a higher power and a resemblance to

a well-known brand ('Caprice des Dieux' is a French cheese). ⏱ *30 min. 43 rue Wiertz.* ☎ *02 284 21 11. Admission free for those 14 and above (take ID as under 14s are not admitted). Mon–Thurs 10am & 3pm, Fri 10am (arrive 15 min early). Bus: 95 to Place du Luxembourg.*

2 **Musée Wiertz.** Romantic painter Antoine-Joseph Wiertz (1806–65) was so popular in his day that the government built him a studio in return for his works passing to the state on his death. A bit of a megalomaniac, he fancied himself the equal of Rubens and Michelangelo—though perhaps few others concurred. 'Interesting' is one word you might apply to his work, or perhaps shocking, obscene, sadistic, or erotic. Pictures such as *The Premature Burial* (complete with body trying to get out of its coffin) are the stuff of nightmares. 🕐 *30 min. 62 rue Vautier.* ☎ *02 648 17 18. www. fine-arts-museum.be. Free admission. Tues–Sun 10am–noon, 1–5pm. Closed public holidays. Bus: 34, 38, 54, 59, 80, 95 to Luxembourg.*

3 ★★ **kids Muséum des Sciences Naturelles.** Everybody loves a dinosaur and they have some unique specimens at Brussels' recently extensively refurbished natural history museum. Back on display and better than ever are the skeletons of the iguanodons found at Bernissart, near Mons, in 1870, as well as that perennial favorite, good old T. rex. The fabulous new Evolution Gallery is a 3.8 billion-year journey, which certainly puts mere humans into perspective. 🕐 *1½ hr. 29 rue Vautier.* ☎ *02 627 42 38. www.naturalsciences.be. Admission 7€ adults, 4.50€ children 6–17, free after 1pm 1st Wed of the month and for children 5 and under. Tues–Fri 9:30am–4:45pm, Sat & Sun 10am–6pm. Métro: Trône. Bus: 34, 80 to Museum.*

4 ★ **kids Parc Léopold.** Gently sloping Parc Léopold is so full of trees that the looming European Union buildings get blotted out by foliage all summer. The pond at the foot of the park, fed by the Maelbeek stream, attracts a great variety of bird life from mallards to parakeets; the trees surrounding it were originally part of Léopold II's botanic garden. Industrialist Ernest Solvay (1838–1922) built the **Institut Solvay** here, a complex of five scientific centers that attracted the likes of Marie Curie and Albert Einstein. Today the mix of architectural styles gives it a picture-book feel. 🕐 *1 hr. Rue Belliard. Métro: Maelbeek, Schuman.*

5 **Maison Antoine.** If you feel the need for fuel, go for the best fries in town served with a choice of 28 sauces at this famous friterie. You can take them to the pleasant Chez Bernard at no. 47 to eat over a beer. *Place Jourdan. $.*

One of the dinosaurs in Muséum des Sciences Naturelles.

The pond in Parc Léopold.

⑥ European Union buildings.
For an idea of the sheer size of the
E.U. administration, look at the **Centre Berlaymont,** shaped like a huge
cross of St. Andrew to the north of
Parc Léopold. It was the home of
Europe's bureaucracy from 1967 until
the discovery of asbestos closed it in
1991. Now re-opened, it once again
houses the European Commission,
and with the flags flying out front, it
has become the symbol of the European community. The Charlemagne

*Art Nouveau detailing at No.8 Square
Gutenberg.*

Building next door houses more of
the Commission's huge, and growing,
administration. 🕐 *15 min.*

**⑦ ★ Walking the Art Nouveau
route.** I love the contrasts of Brussels and, within 2 minutes, you go
from something of an architectural
mess to the cohesion of the Art Nouveau style that flowered from the
1890s until World War I. Square
Ambiorix and its radial streets are full
of architectural gems that show how
attractive residential Brussels can be.
Square Marie-Louise, part of the
area's development in the 1870s, has
a central garden with ponds, foun-
tains, and a great view over Brussels.
Wander the streets and you come
across sinuous, undulating ironwork
of balconies and windows; and gems
such as 34 rue Taciturne by Paul
Saintenoy (1862–1952); the Hôtel Van
Eetvelde and Maison Deprez-Van
de Velde, at 4 and 3 avenue Palmer-
ston (designed by Victor Horta);
houses by Armand Van Waesberghe
(1879–1949) at 5, 8, and 19 square
Gutenberg; the thin, oddly embel-
lished facade of the Saint-Cyr house
at 13 square Ambiorix, built in 1903
by Gustave Strauven (1878–1919) for
the painter, Georges de Saint-Cyr;

and the house designed by Paul Mamesse (1877–1956) in 1898, at 103 rue Charles-Quint. Some are being restored; others are crumbling; all are private homes. ⏱ *1 hr.* *www.brusselsartnouveau.be. See Chapter 2, The Best Special-Interest Tours, p 32.*

8 ★ **Casa Italiana.** Cinzia and Luca Forte's Italian deli sells hams and salamis, first-pressed olive oil, and balsamic vinegars to the E.U.'s Italian community. You have to get in early to grab one of the seven tables at the back for a plate of homemade pasta or the dish of the day. *39 rue Archimède.* ☎ *02 733 40 70. www.casaitaliana.be. $$.*

The central fountain in Square Marie-Louise.

9 ★★★ **Parc du Cinquante-naire.** The Arc de Triomphe leading into the eastern museum area of this park is as bombastic as its famous Parisian counterpart is elegant. It dwarfs everything around it, just as intended. The park was the grandest of Léopold II's schemes, a place for the world to marvel at the glory of Belgium. It was to be somewhere to show off the country's industry in international exhibitions,

much as the 1851 Great Exhibition in London had done for Britain. Léopold II commissioned the Parc and its palace to mark the 'Cinquantenaire' (50-year celebration) of Belgium as an independent country in 1880. The original plans for the exhibition halls were expanded in 1888 so that 'all the knowledge of the nation' could be displayed. Today, those halls house the Musées

Flags outside the European Union buildings.

Royaux d'Art et d'Histoire, the Musée Royal de l'Armée et d'Histoire Militaire, Autoworld, and the Ateliers de Moulage. *See Chapter 2, The Best Special Interest Tours, p 26.*

⑩ ★ Maison de Paul Cauchie. Don't miss the exterior (the inside is open only on the first weekend of the month) of this restored Art Nouveau building of 1905 that showcases the architectural and artistic talents of Paul Cauchie and his wife, Lisa. It illustrates why early 20th-century Brussels was such a seductive city. The facade's gilded mural is reminiscent of works by Czech painter Alphonse Mucha (1860–1939) and Austrian Symbolist Gustav Klimt (1862–1918). ⏱ *45 min. 5 rue des Francs.* ☎ *02 733 86 84. Admission 5€ adults, free for children 12 and under. 1st weekend of month and by appointment 10am–1pm, 2–5:30pm. Métro: Mérode.*

Statue in Parc du Cinquantenaire.

⑪ Aux Délices de Capoue. Go on, reward yourself with an ice cream in this tearoom among the ladies who shop and stop here any day of the week. There are 40 different flavors of ice cream to tempt you, from almond milk to mandarin sorbet. *36 avenue des Celtes.* ☎ *02 733 38 33. www.capoue.com. $.* ●

The impressive facade of Maison de Paul Cauchie.

Léopold's **Grand Schemes**

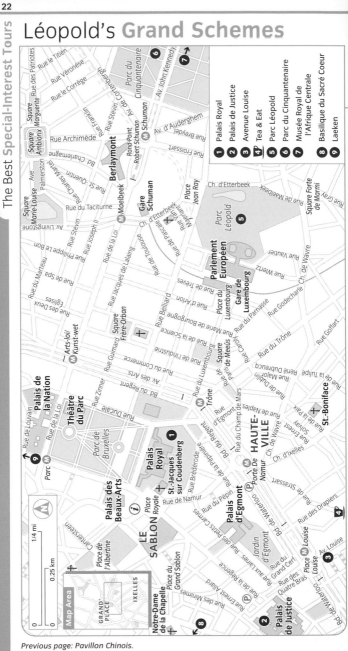

1 Palais Royal
2 Palais de Justice
3 Avenue Louise
4 Tea & Eat
5 Parc Léopold
6 Parc du Cinquantenaire
7 Musée Royal de l'Afrique Centrale
8 Basilique du Sacré Coeur
9 Laeken

Previous page: Pavillon Chinois.

During the reign of King Léopold II, from 1865 to 1909, Belgium grew hugely in power and wealth, based on its enormous coal reserves and African colonies. This tour takes you round the king's most ambitious projects in his aim to make Brussels a world-class capital, having knocked down much of the old city in the process. START: **Tram 92, 94 to Palais.**

❶ ★ Palais Royal. The Palais Royal was originally the work of the Dutch King William I in the 1820s, but it was Léopold who continued the scheme and completed the exterior. You can get a view of posh living, royal-style, when the family is away on its summer vacation. *See p 14,* **❻**.

❷ Palais de Justice. The building of the largest of Léopold's great schemes caused the destruction of 3,000 houses and produced, not surprisingly, a deal of ill feeling. Its architect, Joseph Poelaert, became the most hated man in Brussels and died in a mental asylum

LEOPOLDO II
REGI·BELGARVM
1865-1909
PATRIA MEMOR

King Léopold II surveying his work.

before it was finished, apparently cursed by a witch from Marolles. Opened in 1883, the huge building dominates the surrounding streets with quite extraordinary decorations that trawl the ancient worlds of Greece, Rome, Egypt, and Assyria, giving it the look of a demented dolls' house. See also p 13, **❹** and p 70, **❶**. 🕐 *20 min. 1 place Poelaert.* ☎ *02 508 65 78. Free admission. Mon–Fri 9am–3pm. Closed public holidays. Métro: Louise.*

❸ ★ Avenue Louise. This long wide road, begun in 1859 to join the Bois de la Cambre to the center of the city, was renamed by Léopold II in 1864 after his eldest daughter. A

Palais Royal, built in the 1820s by Dutch King William I.

little farther south from the Place Louise, you can find Place Stéphanie, named after Louise's younger sister, married to Crown Prince Rudolf who died with his mistress at Mayerling. Beyond this, the road disappears into underpasses built in the 1950s and 1960s. The best way to see the Avenue is to take the no. 94 tram from the Porte de Namur to the Bois de la Cambre and back. *See p 94.*

4 ★ **kids Tea & Eat.** This genteel pitstop is full of smart ladies tucking contentedly into sandwiches and exotic salads. There's a great range of teas and a shop selling homeware and deli food. *124 rue de Stassart, Place Stéphanie.* ☎ *02 513 40 00. www.tea-eat.be. $$.*

5 ★ **Parc Léopold.** Originally the property of Léopold II, the park was opened to the public in 1880 after the king's unpopular private zoo was removed. *See p 17,* **4**.

6 ★★★ **Parc du Cinquantenaire.** The park and its buildings were the grandest of Léopold's schemes, showing off the glory of his Belgium. It's a good place for a stroll along shaded paths that lead up to the Arc de Triomphe. The Arch faces Brussels; the eastern end leads into Avenue de Tervuren and the Musée Royal de l'Afrique Centrale (**7**). *See below.*

7 ★★ **kids Musée Royal de l'Afrique Centrale.** In 1885 the European powers handed the Congo Basin to Léopold II, which he treated as his own fiefdom until the State took it over in 1908. To display the riches shipped back from the region, Léopold commissioned the French architect, Charles Girault, to design him a museum based on Versailles and the Petit Palais in Paris. The ornate building, set in the magnificent park in Tervuren, a small town outside Brussels, was constructed on the site of a former palace built by Charles of Lorraine who used it for hunting parties. The museum, opened in 1910, houses an enormous and important collection of items illustrating life in the Congo, taking in everything from giant African insects to a tin traveling case that conveniently doubled as a hip bath; from masks and musical instruments to a remarkable 22.5m- (74-ft.-) long canoe that held 100 men and was carved from a single tree. The museum also contains the complete archives of controversial

The Arc de Triomphe in Parc du Cinquantenaire.

Musée Royal de l'Afrique Centrale houses artifacts from the Congo.

explorer Henry Morton Stanley who helped secure central Africa for Léopold. Although the museum still reflects the way Europe regarded Africa in the past, it's working hard to create a modern ethnographical collection that judges history fairly. Major renovation works begin in 2010, coinciding with the museum's centenary, but the collection will remain open. ⏲ *2 hr. 13 Leuvensesteenweg, Tervuren.* ☎ *02 769 52 11. www.africamuseum.be. Admission 4€ adults, free for children 12 and under, free on 1st Wed afternoon of the month. Tues–Fri 10am–5pm, Sat & Sun 10am–6pm. Closed public holidays. Métro: Montgomery then tram 44.*

⑧ Basilique du Sacré Coeur. Léopold II was never averse to pinching a good idea and his Church of the Sacred Heart was originally planned to resemble Sacré Coeur in Paris. That proved too expensive, and so the design was modified; though commissioned in 1905, it remained unfinished until 1979. A climb to the top of the dome rewards you with spectacular views. ⏲ *20 min. 1 parvis de la Basilique, Koekelberg.* ☎ *02 425 88 22. www. basilique.be. Easter–end Oct daily 8am–6pm; Nov–Easter daily 8am–5pm. Free admission to Basilique.*

Dome admission 2.50€ adults and children. Mar–Oct Mon–Fri 9am–5pm; Nov–Feb 10am–4pm. Métro: Simonis, then tram 19.

⑨ ★★★ kids Laeken. Léopold II wasn't the inspiration behind royal Laeken (the church and château were already royal properties by the time he became king), but the buildings he commissioned here are among the most flamboyant in this leafy royal suburb. The tallest of the royal greenhouses is over 25m (82 ft.) high, while the Pavillon Chinois (originally intended to be a restaurant) and the Tour Japonaise add exotic touches, which astonished the citizens of Brussels when they were built. *See p 74.*

The flamboyant Pavillon Chinois in Laeken.

Le Parc du Cinquantenaire

1 A walk through the Parc
2 Arc de Triomphe
3 Musées Royaux d'Art et d'Histoire
4 Musée Royal de l'Armée et d'Histoire Militaire
5 Autoworld
6 Atelier de Moulages
7 Le Midi Cinquante

Great Exhibitions were all the rage in the second half of the 19th century and King Léopold II made sure that Brussels was not left out. In 1880 he marked the 50th anniversary of the founding of the Belgian nation by transforming a military parade-ground into a grand park with exhibition halls showing off Belgium's industrial and manufacturing might. START: **Métro to Schuman.**

1 ★ A walk through the Parc. Enter the park from the Schuman Métro side and make your way left to the Pavillon Horta, now sadly shut and covered in graffiti. This neoclassical box in gray stone was designed by a young Victor Horta at the start of his career, before he got into Art Nouveau style. Named the 'Pavilion of Human Passions' after the graphic sculpture by Jef Lambeaux (1852–1908) of writhing naked figures that it houses, the building was closed almost as soon as it was inaugurated. The solid

citizens of Brussels proclaimed themselves shocked by the work—which is rich coming from the nation that produced erotic artist Félicien Rops. ⏱ *30 min.*

2 ★ Arc de Triomphe. Totally out of proportion, but as a result rather magnificent, the Arc de Triomphe forms the grand entrance to the park. 300 laborers worked day and night to try to complete it in time for the 1880 deadline, but in vain. Instead a wooden substitute was erected. The arch was finally

The grand entrance to the Parc du Cinquantenaire.

finished in 1910, a year after Léopold's death. You can get into the Arcades, giving great views over Brussels east and west, only from the Army Museum (④). ⏱ *10 min.*

❸ ★★★ Musées Royaux d'Art et d'Histoire. This treasure trove of a museum was founded in 1835. The collection began with the artifacts acquired by the Dukes of

Egyptian exhibit at the Musées Royaux d'Art et d'Histoire.

Brabant and the Hapsburg Archdukes who ruled the country, though some of those early items were inevitably taken to the Imperial museums of Vienna. The museum owns around 650,000 items from five continents, some on permanent exhibition, while others rotate on display. The huge collection (which doesn't include paintings) is divided into four major sections: antiquity, the national archeological collection, non-European civilizations, and European decorative arts. The museum is best known for its antiquity department where I find myself wandering, rather bemusedly, among the wealth of art from Mesopotamia, Palmyra, Memphis, and Rome. When these are exhausted, move on to some magnificent examples of pre-Columbian art from the Americas or textiles and ceramics, which came from China along the Silk Road. The European decorative art section includes Romanesque and Mosan art from the 7th to the 13th centuries plus a good, if currently small, Art Nouveau section. The museum is made all the more intriguing by being something of a maze, and galleries are constantly being reorganized and expanded. 🕐 *1½ hr. 10 parc du Cinquantenaire.* ☎ *02 741 72 11. www.kmkg-mrah.be. Admission 5€ includes audioguide, free for children 12 and under, free on 1st Wed afternoon of the month. Tues–Fri 9:30am–5pm, Sat & Sun 10am–5pm. Closed public holidays. Métro: Mérode.*

❹ ★★ kids **Musée Royal de l'Armée et d'Histoire Militaire.** The enormous collection of the Army Museum takes in 10 centuries of Belgian military history and is housed in the impressive Hall Bordiau, the original building from the 1880s that's notable for its huge glass and cast-iron canopy. Armor, guns, planes, armored vehicles, flags, uniforms, and other paraphernalia show how all-engrossing war and conflict is to humans. The museum is fairly easy to navigate. If the Aviation Hall is open, make sure you see it. It's a huge hall built for the 1910 International Exhibition

and the exhibits follow those 'magnificent men in their flying machines' from Montgolfier and the 'lighter-than-air' craft to the likes of Dakotas, the Tiger Moth, and the MiG-21. Also covered are the more controversial aspects of fascism and the Resistance in World War II. From the museum you can walk onto one of the terraces of the triumphal arch and view the city laid out before you. 🕐 *1½ hr. 3 parc du Cinquantenaire.* ☎ *02 737 78 11. www.klm-mra.be. Free admission. Tues–Sun 9am–noon, 1–4:45pm; Aviation Hall 9am–4:45pm. Closed public holidays. Métro: Mérode.*

❺ ★★ kids **Autoworld.** I'm not particularly interested in motor museums, but this one grabs even my attention. The enthusiast Ghislain Mahy's collection of 800 vehicles acquired over 40 years started in 1944 with a 1921 Ford and includes . . . just about everything. Wander past a little 1896 Léon Bollée, a 1935 Hispano-Suiza, or a 1921 Rolls-Royce Silver Ghost as well as domestic models such as a 1910

The Army Museum is housed in the impressive Hall Bordiau.

Ghislain Mahy's full collection is over 800 vehicles strong.

Minerva that belonged to the Belgian Court. Most of the 300 cars here are in working order. ⏱ 1½ hr 11 parc du Cinquantenaire. ☎ 02 736 41 65. www.autoworld.be. Admission 6€ adults, 3€ children 6–13. Apr 1–Sept 30 daily 10am–6pm, Oct 1–Mar 31 daily 10am–5pm. Closed Dec 25, Jan 1. Métro: Mérode.

❻ ★ Atelier de Moulages. Our 19th-century ancestors had a passion for collecting. In this case, that passion led to the setting up of specialized plaster-casting workshops to produce copies of every major world artwork. During the 1880s, 5,000 casts filled the Hall Bordiau. Today the vaults underneath Autoworld reveal a strange and wonderful world of molds (about 4,000), any of which can be reproduced for your very own

work of art—Michelangelo's *David* is a popular choice for a large sitting room. Prices vary according to size and complexity. You can watch the artisans at work, and sometimes get an impromptu quick tour of the complete collection of molds. ⏱ 45 min. 10 parc du Cinquantenaire. ☎ 02 741 72 94. www.kmkg-mrah. be. Free admission. Tues–Fri 9:30am–noon, 1:30–4:30pm. Métro: Mérode.

❼ ★ Le Midi Cinquante. This cafe/restaurant has a captive audience (it's a hike to find somewhere else to eat) but that hasn't made it complacent. The elegant restaurant serves excellent meals and a good buffet brunch on Sundays. There's a terrace at the front for summer use. 10 parc du Cinquantenaire. ☎ 02 735 87 54. www.restomim.com. $$.

A cast of Michelangelo's David at Atelier de Moulages.

Discovering **Art Nouveau**

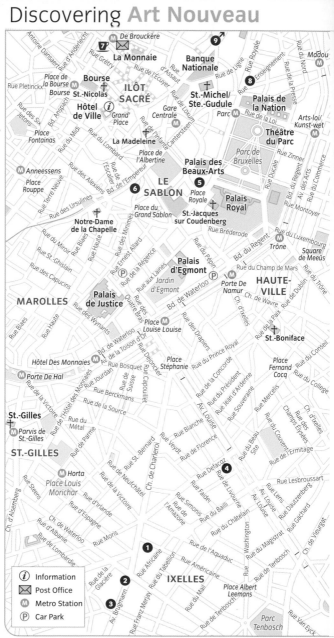

De Brouckère
Rue Grétry
La Monnaie
Banque Nationale
Antoine Dansaert
Rue d'Anderlecht
Rue de l'Écuyer
Rue d'Assaut
Rue de Ligne
Rue Royale
Rue Royale
Rue du Nord
Madou
Rue de l'Enseignement
Rue de la Presse
Place de la Bourse
Rue Pletinckx
Bourse
Bourse
St.-Nicolas
ÎLOT SACRÉ
St.-Michel/Ste.-Gudule
Palais de la Nation
Arts-loi/Kunst-wet
Rue des Six Jetons
Hôtel de Ville
Grand' Place
Gare Centrale
Rue du Loxum
Parc
Rue de la Loi
Théâtre du Parc
Place Fontainas
Rue du Midi
Rue du Lombard
La Madeleine
Rue de l'Infante Cantersteen
Parc de Bruxelles
Rue Zinner
Anneessens
Rue des Alexiens
Place de l'Albertine
Palais des Beaux-Arts
Rue Ducale
Bd. du Régent
Av. des Arts
Place Rouppe
Rue Terre Neuve
Bd. de l'Empereur
LE SABLON
Place Royale
Palais Royal
Rue Montoyer
Rue des Ursulines
Place du Grand Sablon
St.-Jacques sur Coudenberg
Notre-Dame de la Chapelle
Rue des Minimes
Rue Bréderode
Rue du Miroir
Rue Blaes
Rue Haute
Rue du Luxembourg
Rue St.-Ghislain
Rue des Capucins
Rue Ernest Allard
Rue de la Régence
Palais d'Egmont
Rue du Pépin
Trône
Square de Meeûs
Jardin d'Egmont
Rue du Champ de Mars
HAUTE-VILLE
MAROLLES
Palais de Justice
Rue des Wynants
Rue aux Laines
Quatre Bras
Rue des
Bd. de Waterloo
Porte De Namur
Ch. de Wavre
Rue de la Paix
Rue de Dublin
Rue Blaes
Rue Haute
Av. de la Toison d'Or
Rue de Drapiers
St.-Boniface
Hôtel Des Monnaies
Rue Bosquet
Rue Delacroix
Rue Capouillet
Rue du Prince Royal
Place Fernand Cocq
Rue du Conseil
Rue du College
Porte De Hal
Rue de l'Hôtel des Monnaies
Rue Jourdan
Rue de la Source
Rue Berckmans
Rue de la Victoire
Place Stéphanie
Rue de la Concorde
Rue du Président
Rue Jean d'Ardenne
Rue Souveraine
Rue Mercelis
Ch. d'Ixelles
Champs Élysées
Ch. d'Ixelles
St.-Gilles
Parvis de St.-Gilles
Rue du Métal
Rue de Parme
Rue Veydt
Rue Blanche
Rue de Florence
Rue du Beau Site
Rue du Couvent
Rue de l'Ermitage
ST.-GILLES
Horta
Place Louis Morichar
Rue de Neufchâtel
Ch. de Charleroi
Rue St.-Bernard
Rue Defacqz
Rue de Livourne
Rue Lesbroussart
Rue Steens
Rue de la Victoire
Rue d'Irlande
Rue Faider
Rue Simonis
Rue du Bailli
Rue du Châtelain
Av. Louise
Rue Dautzenberg
Ch. de Vleurgat
Ch. d'Alsemberg
Ch. d'Espagne
Rue de l'Amazone
Rue Washington
Rue du Magistrat
Rue Gachard
Av. Louise
Ch. de Waterloo
Rue d'Albanie
Rue de Lombardie
Rue Moris
Rue de l'Aquaduc
Rue Américaine
Rue de Tenbosch
Rue Van Eyck
Rue de la Glacière
Av. Brugmann
Rue Africaine
Rue du Tabellion
Rue Franz Merjay
IXELLES
Rue du Mail
Place Albert Leemans
Parc Tenbosch

7
9
8
5
6
4
1
2
3

(i) Information
✉ Post Office
Ⓜ Metro Station
Ⓟ Car Park

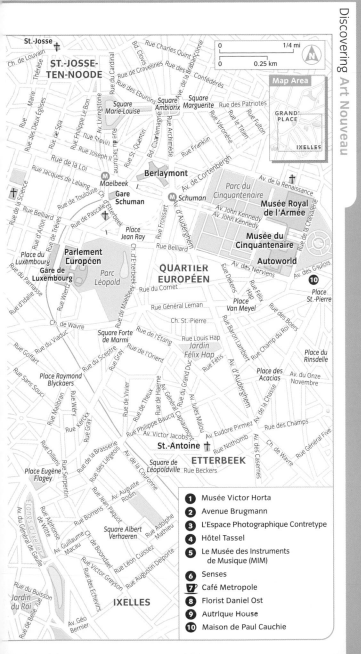

1 Musée Victor Horta

2 Avenue Brugmann

3 L'Espace Photographique Contretype

4 Hôtel Tassel

5 Le Musée des Instruments de Musique (MIM)

6 Senses

7 Café Metropole

8 Florist Daniel Ost

9 Autrique House

10 Maison de Paul Cauchie

Brussels is one of the world's great Art Nouveau cities, but is only slowly realizing the importance of its heritage. Much was destroyed when Art Nouveau went out of fashion and many of the original 2,000 or so private houses have disappeared. There's still no museum to Art Nouveau, and so if you're an enthusiast you have to seek out the treasures on your own. **START: Tram 81, 92 to Janson.**

The former Hôtel Hannon was built in 1902.

❶ ★★★ Musée Victor Horta.
Most Art Nouveau houses are private and closed to the public, but the home and studio of architect Victor Horta (p 33) shows you what an Art Nouveau house looked like inside. It's beautiful and surprising, a place I could imagine living in. Everything was specially designed for the house in Art Nouveau style, down to the smallest detail, creating a sensuous, satisfying whole. ⏱ *1 hr. 25 rue Américaine. ☎ 02 543 04 90, www.hortamuseum.be. Admission 7€ adults and children, 3.50€ students. Tues–Sun 2–5:30pm. Tram: 81, 92, 97 to Janson.*

❷ ★ Avenue Brugmann.
Walk south down Avenue Brugmann to No. 55. 'Les Hiboux' was built in 1895 by Edouard Pelseneer (1870–1947).

'The Owls,' which decorate the exterior and gave their name to the house, are quite charming. No. 80, built by Horta between 1901 and 1903, was the home and studio of sculptor Fernand Dubois (1861–1939). ⏱ *20 min.*

❸ ★★ L'Espace Photographique Contretype.
Once one of the greatest private Art Nouveau houses in Europe, the former Hôtel Hannon was built in 1902 for the engineer Edouard Hannon (1853–1931) by Jules Brunfaut (1852–1942) with furniture commissioned from Gallé and Louis Majorelle. The original contents were dispersed (some pieces are in the Musée des Arts Décoratifs in Paris),

Door knocker at No. 80 Avenue Brugmann.

Victor Horta (1861–1947)

The son of a shoemaker, Victor Horta studied architecture in Paris and then returned to Brussels to work for Alphonse Balat, King Léopold II's architect, most notably on the greenhouses at Laeken (p 76). Influenced by William Morris and the English Arts and Crafts movement, Horta rejected tradition. From his first acclaimed building, the Hôtel Tassel (1893), to the early 1900s, he and his fellow architects dominated architectural style with their Art Nouveau buildings. Horta was more than an architect, he also designed his houses down to the last detail. When the fashion for the Vienna Secession, which began in Austria in 1897 and flourished to 1939, took hold, Horta's Art Nouveau style fell out of favor and he stopped designing private houses in favor of department stores such as the Grand Magasin Waucquez (now the MIM, p 14, ❽). He was made a baron in 1932 and died in 1947.

but it retains the magnificent ground floor, staircase, and fresco. Today it's devoted to regular photographic exhibitions. ⏱ *30 min. 1 rue de la Jonction.* ☎ *02 538 42 20. www.contretype.org. Admission 2.50€; free for children 12 and under. Wed–Fri 11am–6pm; Sat, Sun, 1–6pm. July, Aug: Wed–Sat 1–6pm. Closed public holidays. Tram: 92 to Darwin.*

❹ **Hôtel Tassel.** Every enthusiast makes a pilgrimage to this house, the first building in the world to apply Art Nouveau to architecture. No. 6 rue Paul Emile Janson, with its swirling facade and glorious interior (only accessible on a guided tour, see p 35), made Victor

Replica Art Nouveau treasures can be found at Senses.

Horta's reputation worldwide. ⏱ *15 min. Tram: 94 to Bailli.*

❺ ★★★ **Le Musée des Instruments de Musique (MIM).** Jump on the no. 94 tram in Avenue Louise for the short ride to the Musical Instruments Museum, one of Brussels' great landmarks. Designed by Paul Saintenoy (1862–1952) in 1899, the original store was built by the British company Old England as their Brussels headquarters. *See p 14, ❽.*

❻ ★ **Senses.** I love buying a little bit of Art Nouveau here. Not the real thing (I don't have a fat enough wallet for that), but the excellent reproductions of period jewelry and crockery in this treasure trove of a shop are irresistible. It also stocks stylish modern scarves and bags in Art Nouveau style. *31 rue Lebeau.* ☎ *02 502 15 30. www.senses-artnouveau.com. Tues–Sat 11am–6:30pm; Sun 11am–3:30pm. Métro: Gare Centrale.*

The fantastic view from MIM's balcony.

Art Nouveau Tours

You can find Art Nouveau walks in different sections of this guide, but for expert guidance, take a walk with ARAU (Atelier de Recherche et d'Action Urbaines, ☎ 02 219 33 45; www.arau.org, or book through the tourist office), founded in 1969 to stop the destruction of Brussels' architectural gems after Horta's Maison du Peuple was torn down in 1964. This magnificent glass and cast-iron building, built in the late 1890s as the meeting house of the Brussels' socialists, was undoubtedly one of Horta's masterpieces. Its destruction caused international outrage and radical action. ARAU organizes walks and coach tours, taking you inside many buildings normally closed to the public. For self-guided walks through five major areas, buy the excellent Art Nouveau Walks map (5€) from the tourist office. It covers the city center and surroundings; Saint-Gilles and Forest; Schaerbeek; the European quarter; and Louise and the Ixelles ponds. For another tour, see p 18, ❼.

Horta's Maison du Peuple was torn down in 1965.

7 ★★ **Café Metropole.** Sit in the Hotel Metropole's cafe with the ghosts of Sarah Bernhardt, Isadora Duncan, and Albert Einstein and order a bottle of Champagne. Actually I always go for a coffee because prices are steep at this extravagant tribute to Art Nouveau, built in 1895. There's a great terrace for people-watching. *31 place de Brouckère.* ☎ *02 217 23 00. www. metropolehotel.com. $$.*

8 ★ **Florist Daniel Ost.** Well-to-do Brussels gents once patronized the Niguel outfitter, here at 13 rue Royale, for their trousers and jackets. Originally built by Paul Hankar (1859–1901) in 1896, the shop has a glorious facade and an interior with murals by Hankar's partner, Adolphe Crespin. The florist who now occupies it is one of the world's most admired, particularly in Japan. ⏱ *15 min. 13 rue Royale.* ☎ *02 217 29 17. www.danielost.be. Métro: Parc.*

9 ★★ **Autrique House.** One of Horta's first commissions was to redesign this old house in 1893. It was left to rot until discovered in the 1990s by François Schuiten and Benoit Peeters, today's most influential Belgian cartoonists. Their enthusiasm persuaded the local authority to restore the house which they still administer. Their vision of the place is a dark one; I find its decoration with characters from their cartoons sinister. The house is also used for temporary art and photographic exhibitions. ⏱ *30 min. 266 chaussée de Haecht, Schaerbeek.* ☎ *02 215 66 00. www.autrique.be. Admission 6€ adults and children. Wed–Sun noon–6pm. Tram: 92 to Saint-Servais.*

10 ★★ **Maison de Paul Cauchie.** The architecture of this famous house is more angular than the earlier Art Nouveau style, reflecting the growing influence of the 'Vienna Secession' movement. This new style was less flamboyant and more severe in its decoration than Art Nouveau. It originated in Austria and flourished from 1897 until World War II. Inside Cauchie's house, the tour (first weekend of the month) takes you through the basement and former studio housing paintings by Cauchie and contemporaries and upstairs, which remains as it was left when the painter died in 1952. *See p 20,* **10**.

Facade of Maison de Paul Cauchie.

Gourmet Brussels

Map Area

GRAND' PLACE

IXELLES

Legend:

- (i) Information
- ⊠ Post Office
- Ⓜ Metro Station
- Ⓟ Car Park

1. Cook & Book
2. Dandoy
3. Musée du Cacao et du Chocolat
4. La Maison des Maîtres Chocolatiers Belges
5. Pierre Marcolini
6. Mmmmh!
7. Comme Chez Soi
8. Dille & Kamille
9. Le Café des Spores

Think of Brussels and what comes to mind? Why, good food of course; Belgians have always taken this aspect of life seriously. The capital is one of the world's great gourmet centers. Add chocolate and beer to that and you have all your bases covered.
START: **Métro to Bourse.**

1 ★ **kids Cook & Book.** Take your pick from nine different book-shop-restaurants in one venue. Drink a coffee and nibble a croissant among shelves of comic books in a mock library; try a French novel in a Parisian-style cafe; or take tea and cakes at the long library table in the English book selection. *1 place de la Liberté, Woluwe-Saint-Lambert.* ☎ *02 761 26 00. Métro: Rodebeek. $$.*

2 ★★ **kids Dandoy.** You can't beat the oldest cookie shop in town for their waffles, *speculoos* (Belgian-style biscuits, a cut above), wafer-thin almond numbers, and *pains d'épices* (spiced cakes). Everything in this picturesque 1829 brick building is beautifully packaged, making great gifts. However much I buy here, it's never enough. *31 rue au Beurre.* ☎ *02 511 03 26.*

www.biscuiteriedandoy.be. AE, DC, MC, V. Daily 8:30am–7pm. Métro: Bourse.

3 ★ **Musée du Cacao et du Chocolat.** The privately owned Cocoa and Chocolate Museum, now in its third generation of chocoholic owners, imparts information of the sort to get you through awkward dinner parties. Who first used the cocoa bean? The Mayans, 2,000 years ago. The date chocolate was introduced into Europe? In 1528, when Hernan Cortez brought it to Spain. And so on. It's a delightful place for a quick look at delicate porcelain cups, chocolate sculptures, and even clothes. You can taste at the beginning and watch a chocolate-making demonstration at the end. 🕐 *30 min. 9–11 rue de la Tête d'Or.* ☎ *02 514 20 48. www.mucc.be. Admission 5.50€ adults, free for children 11 and under. Tues–Sun 10am–4:30pm (July & Aug, daily to 5pm). Métro: Bourse.*

The oldest cookie shop in town.

Exhibits go beyond the expected at the Musée du Cacao et du Chocolat.

4 ★★ **La Maison des Maîtres Chocolatiers Belges.** Gain real chocolate credentials with a visit here. Set up to champion artisan, not industrial-made, chocolates, it's the showcase of ten artisans (more will be added) housed in 'Le Sac,' a glorious Grand' Place building. Try a chocolate 'Discovery Workshop' at the weekend and buy a box representing five or ten of the makers'

specialties. To these artisans, chocolate is a way of life, a philosophy, and a manifestation of the Belgian character. *4 Grand' Place.* ☎ *02 888 66 20. www.mmcb.be. AE, DC, MC, V. Daily 10am–8pm. Métro: Bourse.*

5 ★★★ **Pierre Marcolini.** Here's a name to bandy about; the master of haute couture chocolate, a magician who creates masterpieces that he names *tendresse caramel* (caramel) or *sucrette à la fraise* (strawberry flavored) or just Ethiopian iced coffee with Grand Cru beans. The creative genius Pierre Marcolini produces seasonal chocolate collections of the most mouthwatering kind. Extremely expensive, packaged in smart black boxes with silver lettering, they're your entrance ticket to any social occasion. *1 rue des Minimes.* ☎ *02 514 12 06.www.marcolini.be. AE, DC, MC, V. Mon–Thurs 10am–8pm; Fri & Sat 9am–8pm; Sun 9am–7pm. Tram: 92, 94 to Petit Sablon.*

Glorious Chocolate

First, some statistics: Belgium produces 172,000 tons of chocolate every year, much of it sold in its 2,000 chocolate shops. Second, etiquette: take a box of pralines if you're invited to a friend's house. Buy top international names such as **Godiva,** 47–48 place du Grand-Sablon (☎ 02 511 25 37; www.godiva.be), **Léonidas,** 46 boulevard Anspach (☎ 02 218 03 63; www.leonidas.com), and **Neuhaus,** 25–27 galerie de la Reine (☎ 02 512 63 59; www.neuhaus.be), or be a real connoisseur and go for smaller, more recherché names. Try **Corné 1932,** 24–26 galerie du Roi (☎ 02 512 49 84; www.corne1932.be); **Frédéric Blondeel,** 24 quai aux Briques (☎ 02 502 21 31; www.frederic-blondeel.be); **Laurent Gerbaud,** 2D rue Ravenstein (☎ 02 511 57 02; www.chocolatsgerbaud.be); and the delightful old-fashioned **Mary Chocolatier,** opened in 1919 and awarded a Belgian Royal Warrant in 1942, 73 rue Royale (☎ 02 217 45 00; www.marychoc.com). Funky **Planète Chocolat,** 24 rue du Lombard (☎ 02 511 07 55; www.planetechocolat.be) has chocolate-making demonstrations on Saturdays at 4pm.

Mary's is regarded as one of the best chocolatiers in Belgium.

6 ★ **Mmmmh!** Ignore the rather daft name; this is a wonderful store for gourmets, stocking foodstuffs, some pretty nifty (and chic) kitchen equipment, books, and wine under one roof. It also offers regular cookery classes for the amateur chef. *92 chaussée de Charleroi.* ☎ *02 543 23 40. www.mmmmh.be. A, MC, V. Mon–Sat 10am–10pm; Sun 10am–7pm. Tram: 92.*

7 ★★★ **Comme Chez Soi.** Worshippers at the altar of gastronomy should book months in advance for a meal at Brussels' three-star Michelin restaurant. A modest facade gives no hint of the glories within its Art Nouveau, Horta-style interior. *See p 104.*

8 ★ **Dille & Kamille.** This smart shop is a cross between an upmarket lifestyle store and a kitchen supplier. You can find good kitchen equipment, plus all those delightful bottles, cutlery, and table linens to turn your kitchen into something that should be in a magazine. *16 rue Jean-Stas.* ☎ *02 538 81 25. www. dille-kamille.be. AE, MC, V. Daily 9:30am–6:30pm. Métro: Louise.*

9 ★★ **Le Café des Spores.** In this highly original venture, the menu centers on mushrooms—girolles, trompettes de mort ('death's trumpets'), morilles, and more. The cooking is very good; try Saint-Marcellin cheese with morilles or pigs' trotters and finish with . . . yes . . . mushroom ice cream, which works surprisingly well. There's a small select wine list and it all takes place in a delightful wood-paneled room. The chef cooks behind the bar and the place buzzes. In summer eat on the terrace. There's a second mushroom heaven opposite —a small bar where they also run courses on funghi. *103 chaussée d'Alsemberg.* ☎ *02 534 13 03. www.cafedesspores.be. Métro: Albert. $$.*

Everything for your kitchen at Dille & Kamille.

On the **Beer Trail**

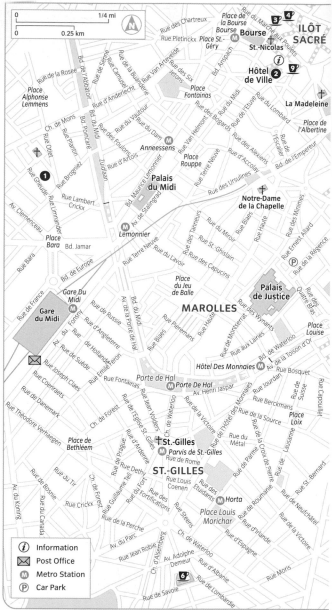

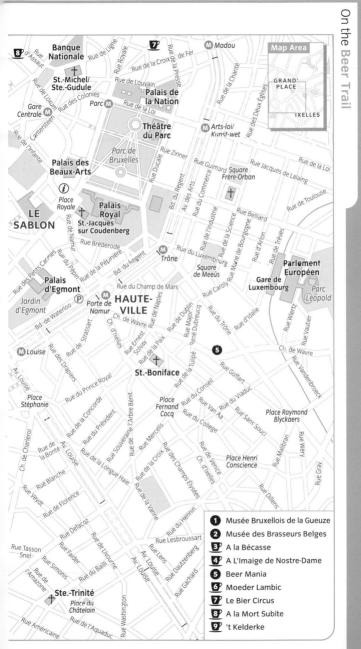

1 Musée Bruxellois de la Gueuze
2 Musée des Brasseurs Belges
3 A la Bécasse
4 A L'Imaige de Nostre-Dame
5 Beer Mania
6 Moeder Lambic
7 Le Bier Circus
8 A la Mort Subite
9 't Kelderke

Beer is to Belgium what Catholicism is to Rome. People make pilgrimages to the country that has 115 brewers producing more than 400 different kinds of beer: 7.2 billion 25cl glasses of it a year. This tour may be an excuse for a beer crawl, but it does take in a few sights as well. So if you want to stay serious, don't drink too much! START: **Métro to Clémenceau or Midi Zuid.**

① ★★ Musée Bruxellois de la Gueuze. A visit to the 19th-century brewery where the Van-Roy Cantillon family has been making Gueuze, Faro, Kriek, and Lambic Grand Cru beers (no joke) since 1900 is a must for anyone interested in the finer points of brewing. ◷ *1 hr. 56 rue Gheude, Anderlecht.* ☎ *02 521 49 28. www. cantillon.be. Admission 5€ adults and children; children under 16 can't drink the beer. Mon–Fri 8:30am–5pm; Sat 10am–5pm. Closed public holidays.*

② ★ Musée des Brasseurs Belges. The only house in the Grand' Place still occupied by the guild that originally built it, now houses the small Museum of Belgian Brewers in its basement. Two rooms in the brick-built cellar provide a brief overview of the art, with traditional equipment in one room and hi-tech machines in the other. The main event, though, is the two glasses of beer (unidentified, because the Brewers' Guild supports all Belgian breweries) you're given by the welcoming staff. ◷ *30 min. 10 Grand' Place.* ☎ *02 511 49 87. www.beerparadise. be. Admission 6€ adults and children; children under 16 can't drink the beer. Daily 10am–5pm. Métro: Bourse.*

③ ★ A la Bécasse. An unsteady step away from the Brewers' Guild, ignore a grotty, neon-signed entrance and venture down the tiny alley to this old inn where waiters pour jugs of beer while you sit at long tables. Try the draught Lambic. *11 rue de Tabora.* ☎ *02 511 00 06. www.alabecasse.be. $.*

④ ★ A L'Imaige de Nostre-Dame. Move on to this atmospheric bar for any of their great Belgian beers. Chimay, Lambic, and Westmalle sit alongside the more common—but no less desirable—Leffe or Hoegaarden. *Impasse des Cadeaux, 8 rue Marché aux Herbes.* ☎ *02 219 42 49. $.*

⑤ ★ Beer Mania. You can find more than 400 beers at this large and extremely well-stocked shop and small bar where you can sample before you buy. It's not only beer on sale, but also the correct glasses to drink each from, and all sorts of accessories to impress the lads at home. *174–178 chaussée de Wavre.* ☎ *02 512 17 88. www.beermania. be. Jan–Nov Mon–Sat 11am–8pm; Dec daily. Métro: Porte de Namur.*

A la Bécasse.

Fruit beer.

6 ★ **Moeder Lambic.** This place is heaving any night of the week with locals and young foreign enthusiasts. Once you've found it (tucked behind St.-Gilles' impressive town hall), grab a seat at the bar, framed with bottles of beer you've never heard of, or grab a table outside and choose your tipple from hundreds of beers. *68 rue de Savoie, St.Gilles.* ☎ *02 539 14 19. $.*

7 **Le Bier Circus.** Here's another Brussels institution with 200 different beers on offer including some serious vintage beers. The new premises are simply decorated and there's a good restaurant at the front and a packed bar at the back. *57 rue de l'Enseignement.* ☎ *02 218 00 34. www.bier-circus.be. $.*

8 ★★ **A la Mort Subite.** This bar is the one no self-respecting beer drinker should miss. It's famous for several reasons: the bar was designed by Art Nouveau architect Paul Hamesse, in 1910, with wood-paneling and mirrors; there's a beer named La Mort Subite ('sudden death'); and this place was a legend even before singer Jacques Brel made it his local. Be warned: the authentic Gueuze it serves can be deadly. *See p 115.*

9 ★ **'t Kelderke.** You need some solid Belgian fare to soak up all that beer, and so descend (carefully) into this medieval cellar for a convivial meal, sitting cheek by jowl with your neighbors. Throw caution to the winds and go for stoemp (mashed potatoes and vegetables) or *carbonnade* flamande (beef braised in beer; also see box, Typical Belgian Dishes, p 118), or just plump for mussels and fries. *15 Grand' Place.* ☎ *02 513 73 44. $$.*

Belgian Beer

Beer and monastic life have always gone hand in hand in Belgium, and the beers brewed at Trappist monasteries are among the country's best known. The famous five are Chimay, Orval, Rochefort, Westmalle, and Westvleteren. In Brussels, you must taste the local brew—Lambic beers—that are produced only in the valley of the River Senne. They're distinguished by being naturally fermented without the artificial introduction of yeast and are aged for up to 2 years. Lambic beer is used to make Gueuze by a second fermentation in the bottle; cherries macerated in Lambic produce Kriek; the addition of sugar and caramel makes Faro. You can see the process in action at Anderlecht's Musée Bruxellois de la Gueuze (p 42, **1**), which is well worth the journey.

The Ninth Art—Cartoons

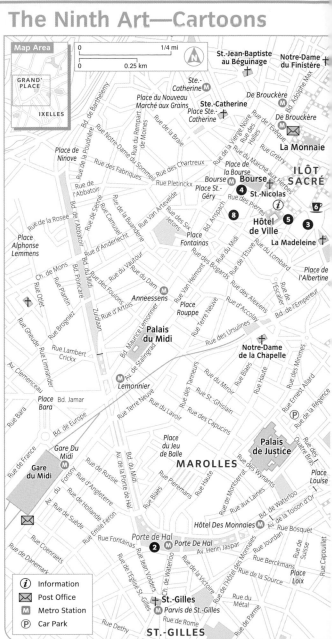

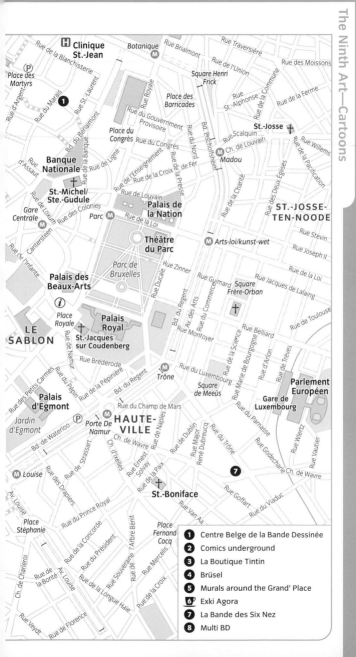

1 Centre Belge de la Bande Dessinée
2 Comics underground
3 La Boutique Tintin
4 Brüsel
5 Murals around the Grand' Place
6 Exki Agora
7 La Bande des Six Nez
8 Multi BD

This tour takes the cartoon enthusiast to Brussels' best comic shops and a museum, and suggests a few streets where giant cartoons adorn the sides of houses and shops. Comic strip art, *bande dessinée* (BD), is as important to this nation as beer and chocolate, as you rapidly discover on this tour. **START: Métro to Botanique or De Brouckère.**

❶ ★★★ KIDS Centre Belge de la Bande Dessinée. What better starting point for a tour of comic strip Brussels than the museum devoted to the so-called Ninth Art? Here you can find the classics, starting with the works of Winsor McCay, moving onto the figures that most Belgians grew up with: Hergé's Tintin and Willy Vandersteen's Willy and Wanda. It's fun from the moment you step into the main hall, where Tintin's rocket stands invitingly at one end. *See p 9,* **❻**.

❷ ★ KIDS Comics underground. Taking the Parisian stance that art should decorate Métro stations, the Bruxelloises have François Schuiten's slightly sinister *Les Cités Obscures* inside Porte de Hal Métro station. Alternatively, leap onto the 1B line, which runs from Bourse and Gare Centrale to Stockel, where you're greeted with the friendlier Tintin on a gigantic mural. ⏱ *40 min. Métro: Porte de Hal.*

La Boutique Tintin. Artwork: © Hergé/Moulinsart 2007.

Thousands of comics at Brüsel.

❸ ★ KIDS La Boutique Tintin. This shop is a must for anyone with even a remote interest in the universally popular hero. It stocks just about everything to do with the comic character, from key rings to clothes, DVDs to books. *13 rue de la Colline.* ☎ *02 514 51 52. www.store. tintin.com. Mon–Sat 10am–6pm, Sun 11am–5pm. Métro: Gare Centrale.*

❹ ★ KIDS Brüsel. This red-brick walled comic shop stocks thousands of new issues. Come right up-to-date with the complete works of famous Belgian cartoonist François Schuiten and comic book writer Benoit Peeters, who created their *Les Cités Obscures* in 20 volumes. Staff are helpful and knowledgeable; they have an English section, and

put on special exhibitions. *100 boulevard Anspach.* ☎ *02 511 08 09. www.brusel.com. Mon–Sat 10:30am–6:30pm; Sun noon–6:30pm. Métro: Bourse.*

⑤ ★★ kids Murals around the Grand' Place. A small area south of the Grand' Place has rich pickings if you're looking for outdoor cartoon murals. *See below.*

Murals Around Grand' Place

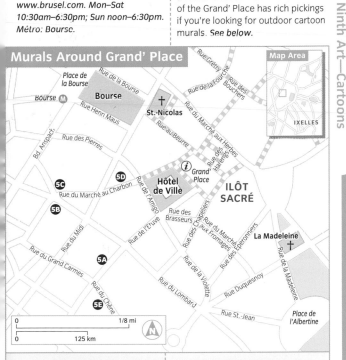

Start at **⑤Ⓐ 37 rue de l'Etuve** for the sight of Tintin, Captain Haddock, and Snowy escaping from a hotel (from *The Calculus Affair*). Tintin was created in 1929 by Georges Remi (1907–83), known as Hergé, a self-taught illustrator born in Etterbeek. In 1946 the *Journal de Tintin* appeared and in the 1950s the stories were published in book form. Today, the familiar quiffed figure is an international character, the books translated into 40 languages with major film-makers ensuring Tintin's continuing popularity. At **⑤Ⓑ 60 rue du Marché au Charbon,** the hero of *Death at the Opera*, Victor Sackville, is seen

against a Brussels background. Author Francis Carin made him an agent in the secret service of King George V of England during World War I. Almost opposite where Plattesteen joins, you can spot **⑤Ⓒ Broussaille,** created by Frank Pé. At the top of the mural, you see the mural within itself. At **⑤Ⓓ 19 rue du Marché au Charbon,** there's a scene from *Les Cités Obscures* by François Schuiten. At **⑤Ⓔ 9 rue du Chêne,** the cartoonist Dany's young, handsome Olivier Rameau maniacally grins at the fabulous Colombe Tiredaile as they grasp hands—and fireworks shoot up to the sky. ⏱ *40 min. Métro: Bourse.*

Cartoonist Dany's Mural at 9 rue du Chêne.

6 **kids** **Exki Agora.** Belgium's response to healthy fast food, but with much more style, this chain of restaurants is just the place for a quick bite (or takeout). Most of these vegetarian outlets scattered around Brussels look like proper posh cafes with well-spaced tables and comfortable chairs in pretty, brick-walled rooms and are open all hours. *93 rue du Marché aux Herbes.* ☎ *02 502 82 48. www.exki.be. Métro: Bourse. $.*

The Cartoon Capital

Belgium is the home of the art of the comic strip, closely followed by France and Italy. An American cartoonist, Winsor McCay, may be credited with inventing the form with *Little Nemo in Slumberland* published in the *New York Herald* in 1905, but it was the Belgians who seized on this new art form and developed it after 1908. Today, the Belgian Tintin, the creation of Hergé, is probably the best known cartoon character in the world. More than 220 million copies of the 24 books of his adventures have been sold worldwide. To fan's undying thanks, the quiffed, cheerful boy reporter—although now 81 years old—always takes then back to their childhood dreams.

Cartoon Trails

The idea of painting murals from Belgium's well-known comics on different buildings was introduced in 1991, starting with a series of 20 works, which are being continuously supplemented. They are scattered around the city, and so you need the map produced by Brussels Tourism (3€ from the tourist office). There are also a number of good books illustrating the works and including maps, such as Thibaut Vandorselaer's *The Comics in the City*, published by Versant Sud (versant-sud.com) and available at all good local bookshops.

Cycling rabbit sculpture outside A la Mort Subite bar.

7 ★ **La Bande des Six Nez.** Run by experts who are always happy to help you, this comic shop offers reductions on new issues as well as stocking secondhand and some collector's pieces in French and Dutch. Their specialty is Tintin from 1950 to 1960, and so you can plug any gaps in your collection. *179 chaussée de Wavre.* ☎ *02 513 72 58.*

www.labandedessixnez.com. Mon–Sat 10:30am–7pm. Bus: 6 to Parnasse.

8 ★ kids **Multi BD.** Two shops belonging to a major comic publishing firm offer a huge choice at reduced prices. Also you can find posters and figures, and readings for young children up to 6 years old, plus workshops on the first Saturday of each month. Both shops (Multi BD for adults and Multi Jeunesse for children) are now under one roof. Check out the website for a list of publications. *124 boulevard Anspach.* ☎ *02 513 72 35. www.multibd.be. Mon–Sat 10:30am–7pm, Sun 12:30–6:30pm. Métro: Bourse.*

Death at the Opera *mural at 60 rue du Marché au Charbon*

Brussels with Kids

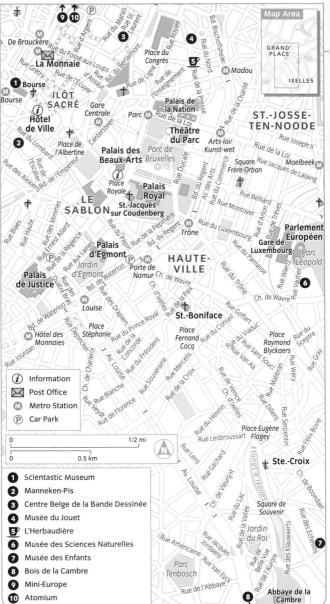

Map Area

GRAND'
PLACE

IXELLES

1 Sclentastic Museum
2 Manneken-Pis
3 Centre Belge de la Bande Dessinée
4 Musée du Jouet
5 L'Herbaudière
6 Musée des Sciences Naturelles
7 Musée des Enfants
8 Bois de la Cambre
9 Mini-Europe
10 Atomium

ⓘ Information
✉ Post Office
Ⓜ Metro Station
Ⓟ Car Park

Brussels is a remarkably good city for children, with a wide variety of museums for every age. Some can seem more like glorified toy shops, and so you have to pick and choose. Or you might prefer to skip the lot and go north to Heysel for the Atomium and Mini-Europe attractions. START: **Métro to Bourse.**

Child-friendly displays at Musée du Jouet.

① ★ **kids** **Scientastic Museum.** This is an unusual small museum in an unusual setting—the Bourse Métro station, which gets youngsters intrigued for a start. Here they can make their voice sound like a duck, or smell their way out of a maze. *Bourse Métro station, Level-1.* ☎ *02 732 13 36. www.scientastic. be. Admission 7.70€ 27 and over, 5.20€ 26 and under. Sat, Sun, holidays 2–5:30pm.*

② ★★ **kids** **Manneken-Pis.** Brussels' best known statue is a sight all children love. Then take them off to the Musée de la Ville de Bruxelles for the little chap's vile costumes. *See p 11,* **⑪**.

③ ★★ **kids** **Centre Belge de la Bande Dessinée.** Tintin is still the major attraction for youngsters here at Belgium's Cartoon Museum, particularly his red-and-white space rocket, but other famous characters are on view, too. Be warned, though, captions are in French and Flemish only. There's a reading section where you can chill out with a book, a brasserie for when youngsters get peckish, and a souvenir shop with a huge selection of postcards, books, and objects. *See p 9,* **⑥**; *p 46,* **①**.

④ ★★ **kids** **Musée du Jouet.** Every child I've seen walk into this cluttered old house stuffed full of

Centre Belge de la Bande Dessinée.

toys is instantly enchanted. It's a glorious, fun, untidy jumble of a place, privately run by an enthusiastic toy collector. Here you stumble across a gigantic tramway, and there are wooden models, prams, and a hobby horse. Steps beside display cases mean that even small children can see inside, and they're allowed to play with many of the toys. There are enough old clockwork toys, trains sets, and dolls' houses to keep parents happy as well. ⏱ *2 hr. 24 rue de l'Association.* ☎ *02 219 61 68. www.museedu jouet.eu. Admission 5.50€ adults, 4.50€ children 4–18, 18€ family 2 adults, 2 children. Daily 10am–noon, 2–6pm. Métro: Madou, Congrès, or Botanique.*

5 kids **L'Herbaudière.** This pretty, family-run crêperie is ideal for lunch after the Musée du Jouet. There's a terrace that looks on to the tree-filled square. *9 place de la Liberté.* ☎ *02 218 77 13. Métro: Madou. $$.*

6 ★★ kids **Musée des Sciences Naturelles.** After a refurbishment, the galleries of crystals and rocks, mammals, and insects now sparkle and buzz appropriately. But the star attraction is its huge Dinosaur Gallery. The museum's collection was always impressive, centering on a set of iguanodon skeletons—herbivores discovered in the mines at Bernissart near Mons in 1870. Their new home is a huge 19th-century glass and cast-iron gallery where they stand, glistening black and suitably scary as they leer at you at head height. There are new interactive exhibits and on-site paleontology and geology laboratories designed as play areas for all children—not just the brainy ones. The Gallery of Evolution is a journey of discovery for all ages. *See p 17,* **3**.

7 ★★ kids **Musée des Enfants.** It's easy to see why children, particularly the under-12s, love this museum, because it's been put together with them in mind.

One of the dinosaurs in Brussels' Musée des Sciences Naturelles.

The views are great from the top of the Atomium.

Youngsters can dress up or learn real baking in the kitchen; there are theater performances, terrific interactive puzzles, painting and modeling, animals, and an adventure playground. Events are in French and Dutch; there's a guidebook in English. ⏱ *2 hr. 15 rue du Bourgmestre, Ixelles.* ☎ *02 640 01 07. www.museedesenfants.be. Admission 6.85€ adults. Wed, Sat, Sun, school hols 2–5:30pm. Closed Aug–mid-Sept. Tram: 94 to Buyl.*

8 ★ **kids Bois de la Cambre.** To get here take the no. 94 tram along Avenue Louise, an adventure in itself for most youngsters. This is the city's most popular park, with lakes and woods, and at the center, a children's playground. *See p 95,* **3**.

9 ★ **kids Mini-Europe.** This is the place to see Venice's Doge's Palace, Brussels' Grand' Place, the Acropolis, Big Ben . . . in fact all the major sights of Europe in one go. As you might expect in this capital of the European Union, the park now includes models of Eastern European buildings such as the three bridges of Ljubljana. The models produced at a 1 to 25 scale fascinate children. If you come during August, they're all floodlit in the evenings. ⏱ *1¾ hr. 1 avenue de Football, Heysel.* ☎ *02 478 05 50. www.minieurope.com. Admission 13.10€ adults, 9.80€ children 12 and under, free for kids under 1.2m (4-ft.) high. With Atomium 22.40€ adults, 12€ children 12 and under. Mid-Mar–Jun, Sept daily 9:30am–6pm, July & Aug to 8pm (Sat, Sun to midnight). Oct–early Jan daily 10am–6pm. Entrance closed 1 hr before. Métro: Heysel.*

10 ★ **kids Atomium.** The Atomium gleams in the sunlight, visible from all parts of central Brussels. The centerpiece of the *Exposition Universelle et Internationale de Bruxelles* in 1958 was designed as a huge version of an iron atom. Whizzing up the central shaft in a glass-topped lift brings you to the Panorama, 100m (328 ft.) up. The views are predictably great; from here you look out over the park to the Brussels skyline. Nearer to hand is the Parc des Expositions, the venue for the World Fairs of 1935 and 1958, the Bruparck leisure complex, Mini-Europe, which looks extraordinary from this height, and the famous Stade du Roi Baudouin, formerly the Heysel football stadium. In the summer, it is particularly popular and you may have to wait up to half an hour. *See p 77,* **9**.

How They Lived

Map Area

0		1/2 mi
0	0.5 km	

GRAND' PLACE

IXELLES

ILÔT SACRÉ
(i)
Hôtel de Ville

Rue du Lombard

Rue des Alexiens

Bd. de l'Empereur

Rue Haute

Place du Congrès
Rue du Congrès
Ch. de Louvain

St.-Josse

Rue de Braga
Rue de Liedekerke

Ch
Rue Willems

Bd. du Berlaimont

Rue d'Assaut

Rue de Loxum

Rue de Ligne

Place de la Presse

Rue Scalquin

Madou

ST.-JOSSE-TEN-NOODE

Parc

Gare Centrale

Palais de la Nation

Rue de la Loi

Théâtre du Parc

Rue de la Chanté

Rue de Spa

Rue Joseph II

Place de l'Albertine

Palais des Beaux-Arts
(i)

Parc de Bruxelles

Arts-loi/ Kunst-wet

Rue de la Loi

Maelbeek

Rue Jacques de Lalaing

Place Royale

Palais Royal
St.-Jacques sur Coudenberg

Square Frère-Orban

Rue de l'Infante

LE SABLON

Bd. du Régent

Rue Belliard

Av. des Arts

Rue du Commerce

Rue Montoyer

Rue d'Arlon

Rue de Trèves

Parlement Européen
Gare de Luxembourg

Parc Léopold

Rue de la Pépinière

Trône

Rue du Luxembourg

Rue du Parnasse

Palais d'Egmont

Jardin d'Egmont

Porte De Namur

Ch. de Wavre

HAUTE-VILLE

Rue du Trône

Palais de Justice

Bd. de Waterloo

Louise

Rue des Drapiers

Rue d'Ixelles

St.-Boniface

Rue de la Paix

Rue Goffart

Place Raymond Blyckaers

Rue du Sceptre

Hôtel Des Monnaies

Place Stéphanie

Rue du Prince Royal

Place Fernand Cocq

Rue du Viaduc
Rue du Conseil
Rue Sans Souci

Rue Gray

Rue Jourdan

Rue Berckmans

Rue Defacqz

Rue Mercelis

Rue Van Aa

Rue Mailbran

Rue Wéry

Rue de la Source

Rue Blanche

Rue de Florence

Rue Souveraine

Rue de la Croix

Rue de Venise
Ch. d'Ixelles

Rue St-Bernard
Ch. de Charleroi

Av. Louise

Rue du Hennin

Rue de Neufchâtel

Rue de la Victoire

Rue Faider

Rue du Bailli

Rue Simonis

Rue du Châtelain

Rue Lesbroussart

Ch. de Vleurgat

Rue d'Irlande

Rue Moris

Ch. de Waterloo

Rue de la Glacière

Av. Brugmann

Ste.-Trinité

Rue Africaine

Rue du Tabellion

Rue de l'Aqueduc

Rue Américaine

Rue de la Réforme

Av. Louis Lepoutre

IXELLES

Rue Washington

Rue Forestière

Parc Tenbosch

Ch. de Waterloo

Rue Hector Denis

Rue Lens
Av. Louise

(i)	Information
⊠	Post Office
Ⓜ	Metro Station
Ⓟ	Car Park

❶	Musée Victor Horta
❷	Musée Charlier
❸	Musée Constantin Meunier
❹	Musée Wiertz
❺	Maison d'Erasme
6̲	Friterie René
❼	Villa Empain
❽	Musée David et Alice van Buuren

Brussels has many museums housed in the former homes of writers, painters, and collectors. This tour takes you to outlying districts, showing Brussels' former character as a series of villages. **START: Tram 81, 92 to Janson.**

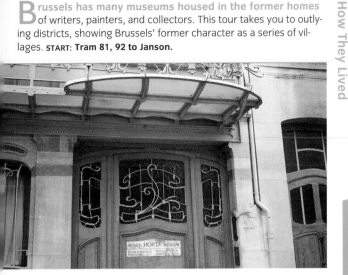

The home and studio of Art Nouveau architect Victor Horta.

① ★★★ Musée Victor Horta.
The house of leading Art Nouveau architect, Victor Horta, is a real jewel. Built between 1899 and 1901 as his home and studio, it's an understated masterpiece. The staircase and stairwell are all wrought iron and mirrors, with a stained-glass canopy. Flowing floral designs on the walls, beautiful joinery and woodwork, and delightful bathrooms all make for a place that feels well lived in. *See p 32,* **①**.

② ★★ Musée Charlier. This delightful museum shows life in a 19th-century, upper-middle-class home. Henry van Cutsem, a wealthy businessman, employed Horta to remodel the house, which includes an extravagant Salon Louis XV room and a Salon Chinois (Chinese Room). Paintings by James Ensor (1860–1949) and Fernand Khnopff (1858–1921) and sculpture by Rik Wouters (1882–1916) decorate the rooms. Opened as a museum in 1928, it's a

door into the past. 🕐 *45 min. 16 avenue des Arts.* ☎ *02 220 26 91. www.charliermuseum.be. Admission 6€ adults, free for children 17 and under. Mon–Thurs noon–5pm, Fri 10am–5:30pm. Métro: Madou.*

③ ★ Musée Constantin Meunier. Social realism became Constantin Meunier's inspiration after he visited Belgium's industrial and coal-mining regions from 1879 to 1881 and saw the workers' wretched lives. The house, where he lived and worked from 1899 until his death in 1905, is full of his often powerful works. I love the rather solid, often heroic statues of the proletariat, but they're not to everyone's taste. 🕐 *45 min. 59 rue de l'Abbaye.* ☎ *02 648 44 49. www. fine-arts-museum.be. Free admission. Tues–Fri 10am–noon, 1–5pm. Tram: 94. Bus 38 to Abbaye.*

④ Musée Wiertz. Antoine-Joseph Wiertz (1806–65) was a universally popular painter in the 19th

Famous Brussels' Residents

Brussels has had its fair share of famous residents, but the plaques marking where they lived are relatively few. In Rue Keyenveld in Ixelles, you find the birthplace of **Audrey Hepburn.** The daughter of an Anglo-Irish banker and a divorced Dutch baroness, the actress lived in Brussels until the Nazis invaded Belgium in 1940. **Jean-Claude van Damme,** the 'Muscles from Brussels' grew up in Ixelles, building up his stamina and strength at karate and ballet school. He moved to Los Angeles in 1981. The mid-19th century saw some of France's greatest writers moving to Brussels, though not necessarily happily. French poet **Paul Verlaine** shot his lover and fellow poet Arthur Rimbaud in the hotel at 1 rue des Brasseurs near the Grand' Place, having bought the gun in the Galeries St.-Hubert, and was imprisoned for the act. **Baudelaire** moved to Brussels in 1864 and proceeded to demolish the country's reputation in two venomous books. **Victor Hugo** spent some time here, first at 26–27 Grand' Place and then at 4 place des Barricades.

century, though he's now almost totally forgotten. His pictures, such as *Burnt Child, Suicide,* and *The Thoughts and Visions of a Severed Head* are pretty gruesome, painted with gusto, or bravado, depending on your point of view. *See p 16,* ❷.

❺ ★★ **Maison d'Erasme.** Man-of-letters Desiderius Erasmus (1469–1536) lived here only for 5 months in 1521, but you feel as if you're stepping into the 16th-century home of one of the most celebrated thinkers of the Renaissance. From the period are items such as the *Adoration of the Magi,* set in a Flemish landscape painted by Hieronymus Bosch around 1495–1500, Gerard David's *Nativity* (around 1480s), portraits of Erasmus, and a library of antiquarian books including some by Erasmus that were censored by the Inquisition. A walled garden with medicinal plants is another delight. ⏲ *1 hr. 31 rue du Chapitre, Anderlecht.* ☎ *02 521 13 83. www.erasmushouse.museum. Admission 1.25€ adults and*

children. Tues–Sun 10am–5pm. Métro: Saint-Guidon.

❻ kids **Friterie René.** Friteries have always been staple snack places in Belgium, serving fries, alone or with hamburgers and sausages. This favorite has been feeding locals for generations. Apart from the friterie, there are two dining rooms, serving mussels and shrimp croquettes. *14 place de la Resistance, Anderlecht.* ☎ *02 523 28 76. $$.*

❼ ★ **Villa Empain.** Art Deco was the inspiration for this villa built for baron Louis Empain by Swiss architect Michel Polak in 1930. The Baron never lived here, donating it instead to the state in 1937 for a museum. But it had a checkered history. It was occupied by the German Army, became the U.S.S.R. Embassy, and was finally privately bought and neglected. In 2007 the private charity, the Boghossian Foundation, bought it and has done a magnificent restoration job. Open for exhibitions to explore the connections between Eastern and Western cultures, the gorgeous interiors, authentically restored, give an idea of the richness of Art Deco in the 1930s. ◷ *1 hr. 67 avenue Franklin Roosevelt.* ☎ *02 534 60 85. www.villaempain.com. Admission 10€ adults, free for children 8 and under. Tues–Sun 10am–6:30pm. Tram: 94. Bus: 25.*

⑧ ★★ Musée David et Alice van Buuren. This is the house of a cultured, rich, and well-connected Dutch banker and his wife. The van Buurens acquired 5 centuries of Flemish and Italian masters as well as 20th-century paintings by figures from James Ensor to Rik Wouters, plus works by G. van de Woestyne, a forerunner of Surrealism. Their elegant 1928 Art Deco house was the social center for the great and good. Composer Eric Satie (whose piano is in the music room), Magritte, and people from political leader Ben Gurion to fashion designer Coco Chanel

The home of the well-connected Van Buurens.

were frequent visitors. The garden is stunning. ◷ *1½ hr. 41 avenue Leo Errera.* ☎ *02 343 48 51. www. museumvanbuuren.be. Admission 10€ adults; garden only 5€, free for children 12 and under. Tues–Sun 2–5:30pm. Tram: 92 to Vanderkindere, Bus: 60 to Churchill.*

Jacques Brel (1933–78)

'Il a chanté le plat pays. . .' ('He sang of the Low Countries') runs the plaque at 138 avenue du Diamant in Schaerbeek, where the famous singer/songwriter was born in 1929. One of Belgium's great heroes, you can see a film on his life at the institution set up by his daughter, **Fondation Internationale Jacques Brel,** 11 place de la Vieille Halle aux Blés (☎ 02 511 10 20; www.jacquesbrel. be), open Tuesday to Friday (and Mondays in July and August) from 10am to 6pm, Saturday and Sunday noon to 6pm.

Fondation Internationale Jacques Brel.

René Magritte

1 Musée René Magritte
2 Le Greenwich
3 Musée Magritte Museum
4 La Feuille en Papier Doré

i Information
✉ Post Office
Ⓜ Metro Station

ans of the surrealist painter René Magritte have long had to content themselves with a visit to his small, two-storied house in Brussels. Now there's a whole museum devoted to the man and his art. Brussels has gone mad over an artist whose life was, despite his work, more provincial bourgeois than revolutionary. START: **Métro Pannenhuis. Tram 94 to Jette Cemetery.**

1 ★★★ **Musée René Magritte.** When Magritte (1898–1967) moved to this small house in Jette in 1930 with his wife Georgette, a less than glittering artistic debut in Paris forced him to work in advertising. By the time he left the house in 1954, he was a recognized and hugely influential artist whose strange images had taken the world by storm. It's difficult to imagine him producing such strange works as *Dieu n'est pas un saint*—a bird clinging precariously to the side of a

shoe—in this house. But he produced half of his output here, more than 800 works in the small, simply decorated set of rooms that could have belonged to any bourgeois Brussels resident, not to one of the most startlingly original painters of the 20th century. 🕐 *1½ hr. 135 Esseghem, Jette.* 📞 *02 428 26 26. www.magrittemuseum.be. Admission 7€ 25 and over, 6€ 9–24. Wed– Sun 10am–6pm. Métro: Pannenhuis. Tram: 94.*

Musée René Magritte in Jette.

2 ★ **Le Greenwich.** If you frequented this old-fashioned bar in the 1930s and 40s, you'd have seen René Magritte and his surrealist friends talking or perhaps playing chess (though Magritte was notoriously bad at the game). Try a beer or go for a simple snack. *7 rue des Chartreux.* ☎ *02 511 41 67. $.*

3 ★★★ **kids** **Musée Magritte Museum.** Opened in June 2009, 40 years after the painter's death, the new museum dedicated to René Magritte is a world-class blockbuster. Housed in a neo-classical 19th-century building, it houses more than 200 works arranged chronologically over three floors. Many people know Magritte's surrealist works and can identify a few of the paintings—those famous bowler hats, pipes, and birds are now universal symbols. But before the museum opened, who knew much about Magritte's life, or who could identify more than a handful of his works? This is a real eye opener, a fascinating story vividly brought to life.

René Magritte

René François Ghislain Magritte was born in Lessines, Hainaut, on November 21, 1898. He studied at the Académie Royales des Beaux-Arts in Brussels from 1916–18, married Georgette in 1922, and worked as a graphic artist doing mostly advertising work until a contract with a gallery in 1926 meant he could paint full-time. He produced his first surreal painting 'The Lost Jockey' in 1927. He moved to Paris, meeting André Breton and becoming involved in the European Surrealist group, before returning to Brussels in 1930. His career continued with major ups and downs, which meant that once again he had to produce graphics to earn a living. He and fellow artists formed an informal group in Brussels, meeting in the modest studio he built in the garden of his house in Jette, or in the bars and cafes in central Brussels. He died on August 15, 1967, and is buried in Schaarbeek Cemetery in Brussels. It was not until the 1960s that his work began to be widely appreciated. Since then many of the images have passed into popular culture.

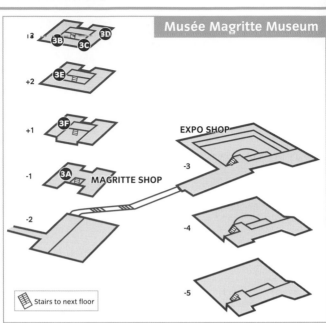

Musée Magritte Museum

Stairs to next floor

Start with the film on Magritte's life on the lower floor. It's long, but it makes the tour much more enjoyable. The audio guide is invaluable. On the top floor, the display on Magritte's early life (1889–1929) takes in works such as **3A A la fenêtre** (1920). More surprising is the range of fabulous posters he produced to make a living, such as **3B Elle a mis son smoking** in 1926. Portraits such as that of **3C Paul Nougé** (1927) and photographs with his friends flesh out the story. Magritte's early years in Paris, from 1927 to 1930 with André Breton and other surrealists, weren't happy but produced new works incorporating words, such as the peculiar **3D L'Usage de la**

parole. Floor 2 starts with his return to graphics at his house in Jette. Then come the revelations and bizarre images such as **3E La Lecture défendue (**1936). The bottom floor covers the later years, with disturbing works including **3F Le Domaine d'Arnheim** (1962). You emerge from the museum wondering why the world looks so . . . well . . . normal. 🕐 *2 hr. 3 rue de la Régence.* 📞 *02 508 32 11. www. musee-magritte-museum.be. Admission 8€ adults (13€ with Musées Royaux des Beaux-Arts admission), 2€ students 18–25, free for children 12 and under, free on 1st Wed afternoon of the month. Tues–Sun 10am–5pm (Weds to 8pm). Tram: 92, 94 to Royale.*

Mont des Arts

The new Musée Magritte Museum, the Musée d'Art Ancien and the Musée d'Art Moderne (which make up the Musées Royaux des Beaux-Arts) are the major cultural attractions on the Mont des Arts, the area linking the Lower Town (Grand' Place) with the Upper Town. It's a wonderful area, with everything within a few minutes' walk and is particularly popular on a Saturday and Sunday. If you want to pack in a cultural day, buy the Brussels Card (p 168) and drop in and out of the museums.

4 ★★★ **La Feuille en Papier Doré.** After a celebration of beer, the surreal nature of this famous cafe, which became the watering hole of René Magritte and other famous artists, could just tip you over the edge. Dating from 1843, this was one of the favorite venues of Magritte and the celebrated Flemish novelist Hugo Claus (b. 1929). Go with the flow, drink more excellent beer, read the odd sayings decorating the walls, and get a proper appreciation of Belgium's idiosyncratic side. *55 rue des Alexiens.* ☎ *02 511 16 59. $.*

Inside the home of René Magritte.

Les Musées **Royaux**
des Beaux-Arts

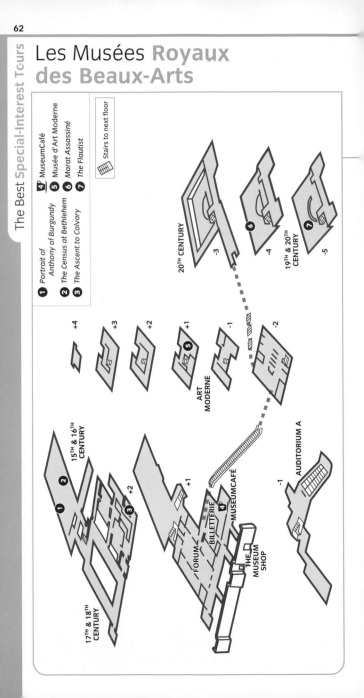

1 *Portrait of Anthony of Burgundy*
2 *The Census at Bethlehem*
3 *The Ascent to Calvary*
4 MuseumCafé
5 Musée d'Art Moderne
6 *Marat Assassiné*
7 *The Flautist*

Stairs to next floor

15TH & 16TH CENTURY

17TH & 18TH CENTURY

ART MODERNE

20TH CENTURY

19TH & 20TH CENTURY

+4
+3
+2
+1
-1
-2
-3
-4
-5

FORUM
BILLETTERIE
MUSEUMCAFÉ
THE MUSEUM SHOP
AUDITORIUM A

The Royal Museums are made up of the Musée d'Art Ancien (15th–18th-century art) and the Musée d'Art Moderne (19th-century onward). The new Musée Magritte Museum (p 59, ❸) has also now come under the same administration. All three museums inhabit the same building and you move easily from one to the next. It's refreshing for a major museum to focus on home-produced artworks. But if you have the finest collection of your own art in the world, why dilute it? START: **Métro Porte de Namur or Parc. Tram 92, 94 to Royale.**

❶ ★★★ *Portrait of Anthony of Burgundy.* Here's a face to fall in love with: the Great Bastard of Burgundy, one of the illegitimate children of Philip the Good who ruled a 15th-century Burgundian Empire that stretched over most of Belgium. Anthony was praised for his bravery and in 1456 given the highly sought-after Order of the Golden Fleece, the chain for which hangs around his neck. It's one of the great Renaissance portraits by **Rogier van der Weyden** (1399–1464), born in Tournai and appointed official painter of Brussels in 1435.

❷ ★★★ **kids** *The Census at Bethlehem.* In one of the world's best-known paintings, **Pieter Brueghel the Elder** (1527/8–69) transposed the Biblical census ordered by Roman Emperor Augustus to tax collection day in a snowy Brabant village (around 1566). It's a masterpiece of detail, from the figures walking on the frozen river in the background to the bleeding of the pig while children throw snowballs. The pregnant Mary rides a donkey in the center of the painting. The museum's Brueghel section also has many copies painted by Pieter the Younger of his father's work.

❸ ★★★ *The Ascent to Calvary.* **Peter Paul Rubens** (1577–1640), the major figure of baroque art in northern Europe, completed this huge, impressive work around 1636 for the main altar of the Benedictine abbey of Affligem, near Brussels. It's richly painted, with light pouring into the picture as the procession makes its way heavenwards. It's just one in the world-famous collection of works displayed here by an artist more associated with Antwerp.

❹ ★ **kids** **MuseumCafé.** Being Belgium, the museum has a very good cafe, overseen by Michelin-starred chef Peter Goossens. Stop for salads, soups, sandwiches, plats du jour, cakes, and some terrific coffee. There's the added benefit of a long terrace with umbrellas to shade you from the sun and a view you can admire for hours. $$.

❺ ★★ **Musée d'Art Moderne.** From the main entrance, take another route into Brussels' major modern art collection, opened in 1984. Mainly underground, the museum circles around a light-well giving natural light to some parts of the collection. Since the Musée Magritte Museum (p 59, ❸) opened, the modern collection has been rehung, and it changes regularly. Although there are enough pictures from the great names of the late 19th and 20th century artists, from Rops and Dubuffet to Picasso, Vlaminck, and Francis Bacon, it's worth spending time on the native-born artists whose works are little known outside Belgium. You access the collection in the same building as the Musée d'Art Ancien.

6 ★★ *Marat Assassiné.* Make sure that you see the most famous image of the French Revolution. Swiss doctor-turned-revolutionary journalist and politician Jean-Paul Marat was stabbed by Charlotte Corday on July 3, 1793. He was a popular hero whose funeral was a cause of huge public emotion. On July 14, 1793, his friend, Jacques-Louis David (1748–1825), was commissioned to paint the scene of his death. The picture is dramatic in the extreme, and its detail completely lifelike. It is hung here in the Modern Art Museum as one of the major precursors of the 19th-century neoclassical movement.

7 ★★ *The Flautist.* The early 1900s saw the flourishing of different styles in Belgium, most notable in the work of Fauvist painter **Rik Wouters** (1882–1916). Wouters' *The Flautist* is a stunningly luminous work where the figure and the background, unusually combined as portrait and landscape, leap out with huge effect. The museum also shows the huge changes in painting that took place

The Death of Marat, *1793 (oil on canvas) by Jacques Louis David (1748–1825). Musées Royaux des Beaux-Arts de Belgique.*

at this time with works by the Brabant Fauvist Jule Schmalzigaug (1886–1917) and Flemish artists such as Constant Permeke (1886–1952) and Gustave De Smeet (1877–1943), who are probably the best known outside the country. ●

Practical Matters

The museums are at 3 rue de la Régence (☎ 02 508 32 11; www.fine-arts-museum.be). It's worth putting aside half a day to visit all the museums. Buy tickets at the main entrance: (8€) for both the Ancient and Modern Art Museums. Buy the special combined ticket at 13€ which includes entrance into the Musée Magritte Museum (accessed from the Royal Museum). Free for children 17 and under, and on the first Wednesday of the month from 1pm. Opening hours are Tuesday to Sunday 10am to 5pm, closed public holidays and the second Thursday in January. Nearest Métro stops are Porte de Namur and Parc, or tram nos. 92 or 94 to Royale.

Saint-Géry & Sainte-Catherine

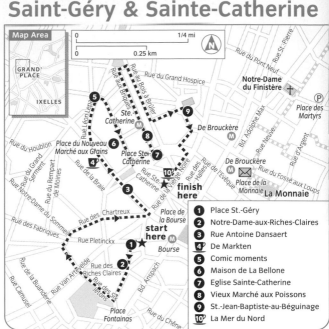

Map Area

GRAND' PLACE

IXELLES

1 Place St.-Géry
2 Notre-Dame-aux-Riches-Claires
3 Rue Antoine Dansaert
4 De Markten
5 Comic moments
6 Maison de La Bellone
7 Eglise Sainte-Catherine
8 Vieux Marché aux Poissons
9 St.-Jean-Baptiste-au-Béguinage
10 La Mer du Nord

Boulevard Anspach once kept smart Brussels safely apart from the working-class areas of Saint-Géry and Sainte-Catherine. Now all that has changed and this part of Brussels is setting the pace with its lively nightlife, designer shopping, quirky shops, and chic restaurants. For a glimpse of old industrial Brussels, walk to the Charleroi Canal. START: **Métro to Bourse.**

Previous page: The Grand' Place.

1 ★ Place St.-Géry. Once the Ile St.-Géry, an island in the River Senne, this is now a fashionable Brussels square. Its centerpiece is **Les Halles,** a 19th-century meat market of glass, brick, and iron, which today houses exhibition spaces and a cafe around a pompous 1802 fountain. The area owes most of its oh-so-cool vibe to entrepreneur Fred Nicolay whose trendy bars Mappa Mundo (p 116), Zebra (p 117), and Le Roi des Belges

(p 116) helped transform the area from shabby to chic. 🕐 **15 min.**

2 ★ Notre-Dame-aux-Riches-Claires. This pretty little Flemish baroque church is tucked away and worth seeking out. It was built in 1665 of red brick, probably by Luc Fayd'herbe, a former pupil of Flemish painter Peter Paul Rubens (1577–1640). Inside it's all weddingcake style and laughing cherubs. Then walk past the **Zinneke Pis,** another of the peeing Brussels' family (this one's a dog), to the next

Notre-Dame-aux-Riches-Claires.

pitstop. ⏱ *15 min. 23 rue des Riches-Claires.* ☎ *02 511 09 37. Free admission. Sat 3–6pm, Sun 9:30am–2pm. Métro: Bourse.*

❸ ★★★ Rue Antoine Dansaert. Once Antwerp was the capital of cool, but now enough top Brussels' names have set up shop in this long street to mount a challenge as Belgium's trendiest shopping city. It all started with Stijl at no. 74 (p 89), which stocks names such as Ann Demeulemeester and Dries Van Noten. Check out Annemie Verbeke (no. 64, p 89), Idiz Bogam (no. 76, p 92), the stunning Natan XIII (no. 101, p 87), and Christa Reniers (no. 196, p 91). Rue Léon-Lepage boasts **Christopher Coppens** for hats (no. 2, ☎ 02 512 77 97), and in the Rue de Flandre, nos. 102–104, **Oxfam Vintage** (☎ 02 522 40 70) takes you cheaply into retro fashion, Belgian style. This store specializes in clothes remade by young designers from fabrics given to them by Oxfam and the results can be spectacular—unique and retro at the same time! ⏱ *1 hr. Métro: Bourse.*

❹ ★ De Markten. The cafe in the Flemish Cultural Center is always buzzing with the young, students, and families. It's very good value (3€–4€ for tasty sandwiches, 7€–9€ for pastas) and is open Monday to Saturday until midnight. *5 place du Marché aux Vieux Grains.* ☎ *02 513 98 55. www.demarkten. be. $.*

Cafe life in Place St.-Géry.

Taking liberties with Manneken-Pis.

5 ★ **Comic moments.** A mural of the philosopher Cubitus urinating, instead of the Manneken-Pis, brings you up short on the corner of Rue de Flandre and the Marché aux Porcs. Comic artist Dupa (Luc Dupanloup) takes the most photographed fountain in the city as the basis for his cartoon, but he's really taking the p. . . . 🕐 *10 min.*

6 ★ **Maison de La Bellone.** It's easy to walk straight past the entrance, and so keep an eye open for La Bellone cafe. Beside it, a passage leads to a well-proportioned aristocratic house from 1697 with the courtyard and entrance now covered over. It was designed by Jan Cusyns, who also helped restore the Grand' Place. Known as **La Maison du Spectacle**, it holds meetings and conferences on the performing arts. 🕐 *15 min. 46 rue de Flandre.* 📞 *02 513 33 33. www.bellone.be. Free admission. Tues–Fri 10am–6pm. Closed July. Métro: Ste.-Catherine.*

7 ★ **Eglise Sainte-Catherine.** The most notable exterior feature of this 19th-century church, rebuilt on the site of a medieval chapel, is the city's last working public urinal. It

The Soldier Pigeon statue on the Square des Blindés.

Christmas in Brussels

Wintertime's Christmas festivities start in the Grand' Place. A life-size Nativity stands at one end while the Town Hall is bombarded with colored lights that change maniacally in time to music—anything from the rock band Queen to opera. It's all rather surreal but great fun and the place is packed. Stalls in little wooden huts sell everything from foie gras (a Belgian Christmas staple) and mulled wine to wooden toys, crystal beads, ethnic clothes, and the like. The stalls stretch from northwest of the Grand' Place to the Bourse and then continue over in Place Sainte-Catherine, which is dominated by a large, illuminated Ferris wheel. There's a skating rink in the middle, surrounded by beer tents and food stands, which makes the place a magnet from the first week of December to the first week of January.

looks onto a square that's invariably full of drunks, albeit usually non-threatening ones. Go inside to see the 14th- or 15th-century Black Madonna. 🕐 *15 min. Place Sainte-Catherine.* ☎ *02 513 34 81. Free admission. Daily 8:30am–5:30pm. Métro: Ste.-Catherine or De Brouckère.*

8 ★ **Vieux Marché aux Poissons.** The 'Old Fish Market' was originally Brussels' harbor, where barges and boats unloaded barrels of salted herrings, silk from the East, timber, and grain into the warehouses lining the quays. Names such as *Quai à la Houille* (Coal Quay), *Quai au Foin* (Hay Quay), *Quai au Bois à Brûler* (Firewood Quay), and *Quai aux Briques* (Bricks Quay) give an idea of this long-vanished trade. Nowadays the area's known for its fish restaurants. Walk up the Quai aux Briques to the Square des Blindés. Belgium's was the only military still using racing pigeons in World War II (there's a strong pigeon-fancying culture here), and so a statue to the Soldier Pigeon is logical, if a little unusual. 🕐 *45 min.*

9 ★ **St.-Jean-Baptiste-au-Béguinage.** Like much of Brussels, a few steps lead you away from the action into peaceful spots such as the charming Place du Béguinage. Once Belgium's largest *béguine* community (*béguinages* were semi-religious, charitable communities for single women who had fallen on hard times), it dates from 1250. All that's left of this once huge community are the ghosts and their church, full of baroque architectural details. Ornate cherubs cavort while the 1757 pulpit looks just the place for a thunderous sermon. 🕐 *20 min. Place du Béguinage.* ☎ *02 217 87 42. Free admission. Tues–Sat 9am–5pm; Sun 10am–8pm. Métro: Ste.-Catherine.*

10 ★ **La Mer du Nord.** Join the savvy locals standing at zinc tables outdoors and snacking on the best fresh fish, washed down with glasses of chilled white wine. *45 rue Ste. Catherine.* ☎ *02 513 11 92. www.vishandelnoordzee.be. $$.*

Marolles

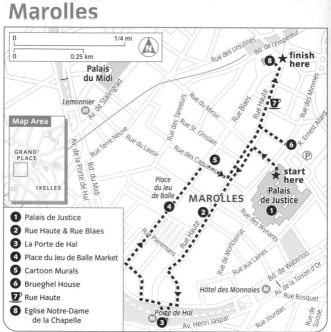

1 Palais de Justice
2 Rue Haute & Rue Blaes
3 La Porte de Hal
4 Place du Jeu de Balle Market
5 Cartoon Murals
6 Brueghel House
7 Rue Haute
8 Eglise Notre-Dame de la Chapelle

Marolles is changing fast, too fast for some in this once solidly working-class district. The Marollien dialect, or *Brusselse sproek,* is now rarely heard. Today old-fashioned cafes sit alongside contemporary restaurants and antique shops defend their territory against the growing number of boutiques. **START: Métro to Louise, and then from Place Poelaert take the glass lift down to Marolles.**

1 ★ **Palais de Justice.** One of the landmarks of Brussels (although regarded without much affection), the Palais de Justice was built on 'Gallows Hill' and had the distinction of being among the largest buildings built in 19th-century Europe (it's larger than St. Peter's basilica in Rome). The proportions are impressive: the dome rises to 105m (345 ft.), it covers an area 551m by 170m (1809 ft. by 558 ft.), and has 164 staircases with 5,671 steps. Commissioned by Léopold II, many working-class homes were demolished to make room for this huge building, and Joseph Poelaert earned himself the title the 'crooked architect' for his mean-spirited eviction of the residents (see box A Little Marolles History, p 73). The location for the court is significant. For centuries it was the place of public executions, serving as a reminder to the working-class Marolles residents of the often brutal power of the State. *See p 13,* 4 *and p 23,* 2.

Find an array of unusual goods at the Place du Jeu de Balle Market.

2 ★★ **Rue Haute & Rue Blaes.** I love wandering along Rue Haute and Rue Blaes and the small streets that run between them, particularly at the weekends when the *bon chic, bon genre* (young and fashionable) Bruxellois descend on the area to shop for essential household items in slightly rough surroundings. You want an ecclesiastical stone carving, a 1920s cocktail dress, a candlestick that's a little different, or a fairground carousel? This is the place. Try **Passage 125** (p 87) for an extraordinary mix of some 30 dealers selling . . . just about everything; **Modes** at 164 rue Blaes (p 92) for top vintage clothing and accessories; **Stef's antiekwinkel** at 63 rue Blaes (www.stefantiek.com) for that carousel (and more); and **New Dewolf** at 91 rue Haute, (www.newdewolf.be) particularly at Christmas, for its range of trinkets and gift items. ⏱ *2 hr.*

3 ★ **kids La Porte de Hal.** Part of the second wall that had protected Brussels since the 14th century, the Porte de Hal (Hal's Gatehouse) was only saved because

of its use as a prison. King Joseph II dismantled the rest when he realized that walled defenses were useless against the new 18th-century weaponry. The gatehouse now houses arms and armor and changing exhibitions and offers great views from its high tower. ⏱ *45 min. Porte de Hal.* ☎ *02 533 34 50. www.kmkg.be. Admission 5€ adults, 4€ children 13–17, free for children 12 and under, free on 1st Weds afternoon of the month. Tues–Fri 9am–5pm; Sat & Sun 10am–5pm. Métro: Porte de Hal.*

4 ★★★ **Place du Jeu de Balle Market.** This long-standing flea market operates every day from 7am to 2pm, but the best times to come are on a Saturday or Sunday morning, when the whole square is chock-a-block with dealers selling a bewildering array of items. I always manage to buy something unsuitable in a fit of misplaced enthusiasm, and then settle down in one of the cafes around the square, trying to get the hang of the indecipherable Marolles slang. The best hangout is **De Skieven Architekt,** 50

Cartoon mural.

place du Jeu de Balle (☎ 02 514 43 69), where the range of beers is memorable. ⏱ *2 hr.*

⑤ ★ kids Cartoon Murals. Cartoon fans come to this area for the murals painted on the houses. On the side of 91 rue des Minimes, Lucifer and St. Peter are surrounded by unlikely characters such as lawyers and policemen; 13 rue des Capucins offers the unusual sight of Laurent-Verron's cartoon missionary, Odilon Verjus, helping the famous (real-life) singer Josephine Baker; while at no. 15 a cartoon by Jijé (Joseph Gillain) depicts his characters Blondin and Cirage. ⏱ *20 min.*

⑥ Brueghel House. In the 16th century, Marolles was a thriving community, so much so that the great Flemish painter, Pieter Brueghel the Elder (around 1525–69), came to live here when he moved from Antwerp in 1563. Brueghel was a cultivated and educated man who counted some of the great and the good in the Low Countries among his friends. During his 6 years in Brussels, Brueghel produced some of his greatest landscapes and scenes of peasant life.

His two sons, Pieter Brueghel the Younger (1564–1638) and Jan Brueghel (1568–1625), were born here. All three were painters, though the Younger Brueghel's work mainly consisted of copies of his father's exceptional religious and peasant scenes. Jan was nicknamed 'Velvet' because of the fluidity and gentleness of his flower paintings. Works by all three artists are on show at the Musées Royaux des Beaux-Arts (p 14). It isn't certain whether the Brueghels lived at no. 132, but the house shows what buildings in this once prosperous area looked like in the 16th and 17th centuries. ⏱ *10 min. 132 rue Haute.*

⑦ Rue Haute. You'll need a substantial bite after all that shopping. If you're after lunch in an authentic Marolles cafe, try a *carbonnade* (stew) flavored with faro beer at **Brasserie Ploegmans,** 148 rue Haute (☎ 02 503 21 24; $$). Or go for the popular, friendly, and retro-styled **La Cantine de la Ville** where a terrace invites you to linger in the summer. *72 rue Haute.* ☎ 02 512 88 98. $$.

Brasserie Ploegmans in Rue Haute, Marolles.

Eglise Notre-Dame de la Chapelle.

8 ★★ Eglise Notre-Dame de la Chapelle. The former parish church in which Pieter Brueghel the Elder was married and buried is a magnificent mish-mash of architectural styles: Romanesque, Gothic, and baroque all make an appearance. The interior is equally glorious, with sculptures of the apostles on the nave's columns, and an ornate pulpit that doubtless held the attention of churchgoers during some interminable sermons. ⏱ *20 min. Place de la Chapelle.* ☎ *02 512 07 37. Free admission. Mon–Fri 9:30am–4:30pm; Sat 12:30–5pm; Sun 8am–7:30pm. Métro: Gare Centrale.*

A Little Marolles History

Marolles was originally built up in the 17th century, for the artisans who served the nearby rich in the Sablon district. Strictly speaking, it occupies the area at the foot of the Galgenberg (Gallows) hill where the Palais de Justice stands. Huge swathes of houses were destroyed to accommodate the base of this hated and massive structure; the architect Joseph Poelaert earned the name *de skieven architek* (the crooked architect), due to his habit of using the police to forcibly drive the Marolles inhabitants out of their homes. In 1860, the River Senne was vaulted over and the old textile industries that had lined its banks and given the inhabitants their living were closed or moved on. The area went further downhill, to be revived in the 1980s. Its own dialect, *Brusselse Sproek* or *Marollien,* is totally indecipherable to foreigners (which covers everyone not born in the Marolles), which is probably a good thing because it's richly abusive. For a taste of the language, visit the Théâtre Royal de Toone (p 126), which puts on puppet plays in the dialect.

Royal Laeken

- ① Notre-Dame de Laeken
- ② Cimetière de Laeken
- ③ Jardin du Fleuriste
- ④ Château Royal
- ⑤ Serres Royales
- ⑥ Pavillon Chinois
- ⑦ Tour Japonaise
- ⑧ Parc d'Osseghem
- ⑨ Atomium
- 🔟 Atomium Restaurant

Laeken is the home of Belgium's royal family. Their palace nestles in a green hilly park. To the north stands the Art Deco Grand Palais, the major trade fair venue of the Parc des Expositions. This is a longish excursion, so take good walking shoes and, if it's a fine day, a picnic. **START: Métro to Bockstael, and then left along Rue Léopold I to Parvis Notre-Dame (about 10 minutes' walk).**

① ★ Notre-Dame de Laeken.
Begun in 1854 to designs by Joseph Poelaert as a memorial to Queen Louise-Marie after her death in 1850, the church of Our Lady of Laeken was redesigned in 1865 and only completed between 1904 and 1922. It's a huge neo-Gothic monstrosity, notable for its Royal Crypt that houses almost every member of the Belgian royal family since Queen Louise-Marie. ⏱ *20 min. Parvis Notre-Dame.* ☎ *02 479 23 63. Free admission. Tues–Sun 2–5pm,*

Crypt Sun 2–5pm and royal anniversaries. Métro: Bockstael.

② ★ kids Cimetière de Laeken.
Walk past the monument to French soldiers killed in Belgium in World War I, and then through the gates into this crowded cemetery. The crumbling tombs and statues leaning at odd angles give the place a desolate feel. Like all old cemeteries it has a melancholy romanticism, highlighted on June 21, midsummer, when the sun's rays appear in the shape of a heart inside the small

Explore the unusual gravestones in Laeken's cemetery.

mausoleum of one Léonce Evrard in the Grande Avenue. He lies here surrounded by the great and the good of Brussels, now mainly forgotten except for figures such as architect Joseph Poelaert (1817–79), painter Fernand Khnopff (1858–1921), and playwright Michel de Ghelderode (1898–1962). At the eastern side of the cemetery, just by a ruined chapel, the first version of Auguste Rodin's *The Thinker* sits in an attitude of eternal contemplation on the tomb of art critic Josef Dillen. 🕐 *20 min. Parvis Notre-Dame.* ☎ *02 513 89 40. Free admission. Tues–Sun 8:30am–4:30pm. Daily Sept 30–Nov 15. Métro: Bockstael.*

❸ ★ **kids** **Jardin du Fleuriste.** The 'Florist's Garden,' in the grounds beside Léopold II's Stuyvenberg estate, is a real discovery. When the former royal estates were made into public parks in the 1950s, these 4 hectares (almost 10 acres) lay forgotten and neglected until 1999, when they were brought back to life. The garden is a mixture of formal design and planting, dotted with contemporary sculpture, and offering views over Brussels. It's an educational exercise in the gardens and plantings of the past. From here you can walk down to the Sobieski Park with its children's playground. 🕐 *30 min. Avenue des Robiniers.* ☎ *02 775 75 11. Free admission. Daily Apr 8am–6:30pm; May–Aug 8am–8pm; Sept 8am–7pm; Oct–Mar 8am–5:30pm. Métro: Stuyvenbergh.*

Standing guard at the entrance to the Château Royal.

❹ **Château Royal.** A walk along Avenue du Parc Royal brings you to the main entrance (and the nearest you can get) to the modest royal palace, originally called Schoonberg. It was built in 1782–4 for the Austrian Governor General who then ruled the country. Subsequently abandoned, the house was restored in 1804 by French Emperor Napoleon who briefly occupied it, and most notably planned his disastrous Russian military campaign from here. After a fire in 1890, it was rebuilt along its original Louis XV architectural lines. Turn around, and you can see the white stone neo-Gothic monument to Léopold I at the other end of the Avenue de la Dynastie, which runs from the palace to the statue. ⏱ *20 min.*

⑤ Serres Royales. The tops of these magnificent glasshouses are all you can see from the outside, unless you're lucky enough to be in Brussels in spring when they briefly open to the public. The 11 linked greenhouses were built for King Léopold II by Alphonse Balat and the young Victor Horta in the 1870s: Some of the tropical plants date back to the 19th century. Léopold so loved the greenhouses that he had himself moved here on his deathbed. ⏱ *2 hr. (for a visit in spring). 61 avenue du Parc Royal.* ☎ *02 513 89 40. www.monarchie. be. 3 weeks Apr–May only. Prices and times vary. Métro: Houba Brugmann.*

⑥ ★ Pavillon Chinois. Around the corner past the Fontaine de Neptune (Neptune's Fountain) are two of Léopold II's most exotic fantasies. After seeing the east Asian designs at the 1900 Paris Exhibition, the king commissioned French specialist, Alexandre Marcel (1860–1928), to draw up plans for Chinese and Japanese buildings. Designed in 1901–2, the main parts of the Chinese Pavilion were made in Shanghai, and finally put together here in 1910. Now with its polychrome gloriously restored, it contains Chinese porcelain and furniture. *See* **⑦**.

⑦ ★ Tour Japonaise. This five-tiered Japanese Tower was based on a 17th-century Buddhist pagoda, and constructed mainly in Japan before being shipped to the 1900 Paris Exhibition. Léopold then purchased the building and shipped it to Laeken. You can only access the exhibition of Japanese art, porcelain, and armor, and the staircase, a glorious mix of Art Nouveau and Japanese styles. The stained glass and chandelier were created by French artists inspired by Japanese design. ⏱ *45 min. 44 avenue J Van Praet.* ☎ *02 268 16 08. www.mrah. be. Admission includes both Pavillon*

Children will enjoy Sobieski Park next to the Jardin du Fleuriste.

Alexandre Marcel's elaborate Chinese Pavilion designed for King Léopold II.

Chinois and Tour Japonaise: 4€ adults, 3€ children 13–17, free for children 12 and under. Tickets from Tour Japonaise. Tues–Fri 9:30am–5pm; Sat & Sun 10am–5pm. Tram: 4, 23; bus: 53 to Araucaria.

8 ★ kids **Parc d'Osseghem.** The 15-minute walk to the Atomium heads past the noisy canine department of the Brussels police to Osseghem Park, designed by landscape architect Jules Buyssens for the 1935 World Fair. Wander through alleys of beech trees to a little pond complete with bridges and an open-air amphitheater. ⏲ 20 min.

9 ★ kids **Atomium.** You can't miss this centerpiece of the 1958 *Exposition Universelle et Internationale de Bruxelles*, which still dominates the city skyline. It's a giant stylized model of an iron atom, enlarged 165 billion times. Reopened in February 2006 after refurbishment, its nine huge steel balls are connected by metal tubes. The main pull is the view: take a lift to the top, though in summer it can take at least half an hour because queues are long and the lift small. ⏲ 1–2 hr., depending on season. Square de l'Atomium. ☎ 02 475 47 75. www.atomium.be. Admission

11€ adults, 5€ children 12–18, 4€ children 6–11, free for children 5 and under. Daily 10am–6pm. Métro: Heysel. Tram: 19, 21, 81.

10 ★ kids **Atomium Restaurant.** Prices may be high, but they are justified by the views and the good food. It's self-service with a wide lunchtime selection by day and a gourmet restaurant by night (book ahead). ☎ 02 479 57 50. www.belgiumtaste.com. Daily 10am–6pm & 7:30pm–11pm. $$.

The Atomium can't be missed.

Ixelles

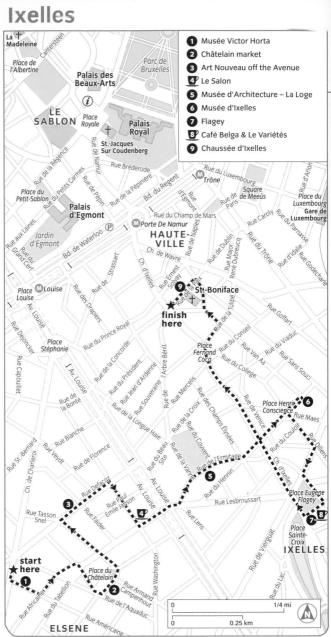

1 Musée Victor Horta
2 Châtelain market
3 Art Nouveau off the Avenue
4 Le Salon
5 Musée d'Architecture – La Loge
6 Musée d'Ixelles
7 Flagey
8 Café Belga & Le Variétés
9 Chaussée d'Ixelles

La Madeleine
Place de l'Albertine
Cantersteen
Parc de Bruxelles
Palais des Beaux-Arts
ⓘ
LE SABLON
Place Royale
Palais Royal
St.-Jacques Sur Coudenberg
Rue de Namur
Rue de la Régence
Rue Bréderode
Ⓜ Trône
Rue du Luxembourg
Place du Petit-Sablon
Rue des Petits Carmes
Rue de Pepin
Palais d'Egmont
Jardin d'Egmont
Rue aux Laines
Rue du Grand Cerf
Bd. de Waterloo
Ⓟ
Porte De Namur Ⓜ
HAUTE-VILLE
Ch. de Wavre
Rue d'Egmont
Rue de Naples
Rue de Paris
Square de Meeûs
Place du Luxembourg
Gare de Luxembourg
Rue d'Arlon
Rue Caroly
Rue du Parnasse
Rue du Trône
Rue Major René Dubreucq
Rue de Dublin
Rue d'Idalie
Rue Godecharle
Place Louise Ⓜ
Rue des Drapiers
Rue du Prince Royal
Rue Ernest Solvay
9 St-Boniface
★ finish here
Rue de la Tulipe
Rue Goffart
Rue du Viaduc
Rue Sans Souci
Place Stéphanie
Rue Dejoncker
Av. Louise
Rue de la Concorde
Rue du Président
Rue Jean d'Ardenne
Rue Souveraine
Rue de l'Arbre Bénit
Place Fernand Cocq
Rue du Collège
Rue du Conseil
Rue Van Aa
Av. Louise
Rue de la Bonté
Rue de la Longue Haie
Rue Mercelis
Rue des Champs Élysées
Place Henri Conscience 6
Rue Maes
Rue de Venise
Ch. de Charleroi
Rue St.-Bernard
Rue Veydt
Rue Blanche
Rue de Florence
Rue du Beau Site
Rue de la Croix
Rue du Couvent
Rue de l'Ermitage
5
Rue du Coulon
Rue Dillens
Ch. d'Ixelles
Rue Capouillet
3
Rue Tasson Snel
Rue Defacqz
Rue Paul Emile Janson
Rue Faider
4
Av. Louise
Rue du Hennin
Rue Lesbroussart
Rue Lens
Place Eugène Flagey
7 8
Place Sainte-Croix
IXELLES
start here ★
1
Rue Africaine
Rue du Tabellion
Place du Châtelain
2
Rue Armand Campenhout
Rue de l'Aquaduc
Rue Washington
Rue Américaine
Rue de Vergnies
Rue du Lac

ELSENE

0 _____ 1/4 mi
0 _____ 0.25 km
Ⓝ

One of the city's liveliest outlying areas, Ixelles is a mix of styles—from the beauty of Art Nouveau to the vibrant life of the African Matongé district. It's divided into east and west by posh Avenue Louise (top designer names and local grandees), but Bohemia lurks in the increasingly smart and sought-after western end around Saint-Gilles. START: **Tram 81 to Horta.**

Sgraffito panel at the Hôtel Ciamberlani by Paul Hankar.

❶ ★★★ Musée Victor Horta. Victor Horta lived here from the end of the 19th century to 1919, designing both the house and its interior down to the smallest detail. It's a must for anyone interested in Art Nouveau. The rooms run off a glorious, curving staircase, lit by a skylight. He also collected the works of his contemporaries: there are paintings by Félicien Rops (1833–98) and Joseph Heymans (1839–1921). ⏱ *1 hr. See p 32,* ❶.

❷ ★ Châtelain market. It's a short walk to place du Châtelain and the Wednesday market (2–7pm), which attracts both locals and gourmets from farther afield for the homemade cheeses, cakes, and pastries. ⏱ *10 min.*

❸ ★★ Art Nouveau off the Avenue. There are Art Nouveau treasures just off the Avenue Louise, where a short detour brings you to the **Hôtel Tassel** at 6 rue Paul-Emile Janson, the 1897 house that established Horta's fame. At the same

time, fellow architect and friend Paul Hankar (1849–1901) was designing his own house and studio, the **Hôtel Hankar,** at 71 rue Defacqz. It's noted for its four *sgraffito*-decorated panels of morning, afternoon, evening, and night (see p 82). A little farther along at no. 48 you come across the handsome red brick **Hôtel Ciamberlani,** again designed by Paul Hankar in 1897 for the Belgian painter, Albert Ciamberlani (1864–1956). ⏱ *15 min.*

The home and studio of Paul Hankar.

Africa & Beyond in Brussels

The Matongé is a colorful, vibrant area of Brussels, running down from Porte de Namur in Ixelles along Chaussée de Wavre and Rue du Trône to the west and the east. Named after an area of Kinshasa in the Congo, its roots lie in the students who came here from Africa after Congolese independence in the 1950s to study at the Free University of Brussels. Today it's a busy, lively part of Brussels, well worth a walk through. It's the place for exotic vegetables, African fabrics, clothes, street snacks, and particularly music. Your best bet here is **Musicanova** (☎ 02 511 66 94) at no. 24 in the shabby surroundings of the Galerie d'Ixelles. Pick up a snack from places selling street food such as chicken piri-piri; otherwise walk down the pedestrianized section of Rue Longue Vie where you can roll in and out of the African and Indian bars and restaurants until the small hours. For a more upmarket experience, try **L'Horloge du Sud** (p 104) for plantains and *Yassa* (chicken marinated in limes and cooked with onions), and impromptu music sessions. The area's June weekend festival, **Matongé en Couleurs,** is a must (information from the Tourist Office, p 164).

4 **Le Salon.** A local, old-fashioned, favorite among the well-heeled, rather sedate residents, this eaterie is a great place for tea and cakes. *3–5 rue du Bailli.* ☎ *02 648 65 39. $.*

5 ★ **Musée d'Architecture—La Loge.** The architectural museum is mainly aimed at specialists, putting on in-depth temporary exhibitions of Brussels' architectural heritage. Housed in a former Masonic lodge, it's also one of

The Musée d'Ixelles houses some real trasures.

Classical music venue Flagey.

Europe's major archives, used by professional architects and students from across the continent. The **Fondation pour l'Architecture** opposite (55 rue de l'Ermitage; www. foundationpourlarchitecture.be) works with the museum on public exhibitions. ⏱ *45 min. 86 rue de l'Ermitage.* ☎ *02 642 24 62. www. aam.be. Admission 4€ adults, 2€ students, 1€ children 6–12. Tues–Sun noon–6pm; Wed to 9pm. Bus: 71 to Flagey.*

❻ ★★ Musée d'Ixelles. There's more Art Nouveau architecture where Rue de l'Ermitage meets Rue des Champs Elysées. Nos. 72 and 74 were built in the early 1900s by Paul Hamesse (1877–1956) and Léon Delune (1862–1941). Walk up Rue Jean Van Volsem for a real gem: the Ixelles Museum was founded in 1892 with a bequest from the painter Edmond De Praetere (1826–88). It features mainly modern art, much by Belgian artists. You find

Art Nouveau & *Sgraffiti*

The term *sgraffito* comes from the Italian 'to scratch' and refers to the wall decor technique of applying colors on top of each other, and then cutting away part of the top coat to make the design. It was used on the facades of Brussels' Art Nouveau houses, such as **71 rue Defacqz** (p 79, ❸), **Les Hiboux,** 55 avenue Brugmann, (p 32, ❷), and the **Hôtel Ciamberlani** (p 79, ❸). *Sgraffito* in all its gilded glory covers the outside of the **Maison de Paul Cauchie,** 5 rue des Francs (p 20, ❿; p 35, ❿).

Classic Art Nouveau features on Rue St. Boniface.

works by René Magritte, Léon Frédéric (1856–1940), and Rik Wouters (1882–1916) among the odd Pablo Picasso, Seurat, and Raoul Dufy as well as a large Toulouse-Lautrec poster collection. ⏱ *1½ hr. 71 rue Van Volsem.* ☎ *02 515 64 22. www. museedixelles.be. Free admission. Tues–Sun 11:30am–5pm. Closed public holidays. Bus: 71 to Van Volsem.*

7 ★ **Flagey.** You can't miss the old Institut National de Radiodiffusion (INR), built in the 1930s for the Belgian broadcast media. It was state-of-the-art at the time, with advanced engineering in its concert halls and studios. It fell on hard times when the INR moved out, but was rescued by private entrepreneurs who built a cinema and space for classical music events. ⏱ *15 min. See p 124.*

8 Smart **Café Belga** (18 Place Flagey; ☎ 02 640 35 08; $) is all zinc and chrome, 1950s, and

trendy. It's great for a drink, and swings until 2am. For something more substantial, try **Le Variétés** (4 Place Saint Croix; ☎ 02 647 04 36. $$), which looks like a retro diner. I first discovered it feeling delicate after a good night out and have never looked back. The welcome is genuine, the food restorative, and the customers straight out of central casting.

9 ★ **kids Chaussée d'Ixelles.** There's nothing like a contest to improve an area. A facade competition launched by the Ixelles commune in 1898 produced some classic Art Nouveau houses. Check out Rue Saint-Boniface, nos. 15, 16, 19, 20, and 22, and Rue Solvay (even numbers from 12 to 22), all the work of Ernest Blerot (1870–1957) in 1900. Also look out for no. 32 on Rue Solvay, designed by Victor Taelemans (1864–1920) in 1907. ⏱ *30 min.* ●

The Best Shopping

Brussels **Shopping**

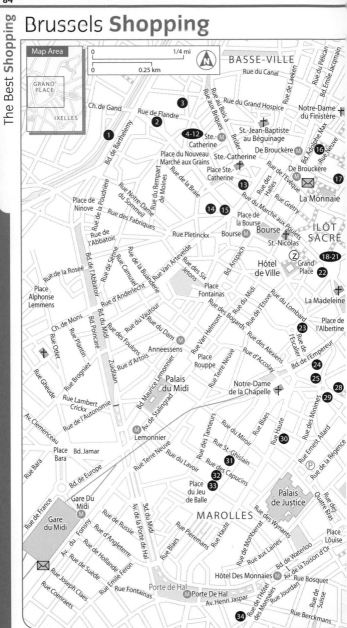

Map Area

| 0 | | 1/4 mi |
| 0 | 0.25 km | |

GRAND
PLACE

IXELLES

BASSE-VILLE

Rue du Canal

Ch. de Gand

Rue de Flandre

Rue du Grand Hospice

Rue au Bois à Brûler

Rue aux Briques

Notre-Dame
du Finistère

Bd. Émile Jacqmain

Rue du Pélican

Rue de Laeken

❸

❷

❹-❶❷ Ste.-
Catherine

St.-Jean-Baptiste
au Béguinage

De Brouckère

De Brouckère

Rue Neuve

Bd. Adolphe Max

❶❻

Place du Nouveau
Marché aux Grains

Ste.-Catherine

Rue de l'Évêque

❶❼

Place de
Ninove

Rue Notre-Dame
du Sommeil

Place Ste.-
Catherine

Rue du Rempart
des Moines

Rue de la Braie

❶❸

Rue des
Halles

Rue du Marché aux Poulets

Rue Grétry

La Monnaie

Rue de la Poudrière

Rue des Fabriques

❶❹ ❶❺

Place de
la Bourse

Bourse

ILOT
SACRÉ

Rue de
l'Abbatoir

Rue Pletinckx

Bourse

St.-Nicolas

❶❽-❷❶

Rue de la Roseé

Bd. de l'Abbatoir

Rue de Senne

Rue de la Buanderie

Rue Camusel

Rue Van Artevelde

Rue des Six
Jetons

Bd. Anspach

Hôtel
de Ville

Grand'
Place

❷❷

Place
Fontainas

Rue du Midi

La Madeleine

Place
Alphonse
Lemmens

Ch. de Mons

Bd. du Midi

Rue d'Anderlecht

Rue du Vautour

Rue du Dam

Rue des Bogards

Rue de l'Étuve

Rue du Lombard

Place de
l'Albertine

Rue Otlet

Rue Plattin

Bd. Poincaré

Rue des Foulons

Anneessens

Rue Van Helmont

Rue des Alexiens

Rue d'Accoly

❷❸

Rue de
l'Escalier

Ch. de Mons

Rue Gheude

Rue Broigniez

Rue d'Artois

Place
Rouppe

Rue Terre Neuve

Notre-Dame
de la Chapelle

Bd. de l'Empereur

❷❹

❷❺

Zuidlaan

Bd. Maurice Lemonnier

Palais
du Midi

❷❽

❷❾

Av. Clemenceau

Rue Lambert
Crickx

Rue de l'Autonomie

Av. de Stalingrad

Lemonnier

Rue des Tanneurs

Rue du Miroir

Rue Blaes

Rue Haute

Rue des Minimes

❸❶

Rue Ernest Allard

Place
Bara

Bd. Jamar

Bd. de Europe

Rue Terre Neuve

Rue du Lavoir

Rue St-Ghislain

❸❶

Rue des Capucins

❸❷

Rue de la Régence

Rue Bara

Rue de France

Gare Du
Midi

Gare
du Midi

Av. du Fonsny

Rue de Russie

Av. de la Porte de Hal

Bd. du Midi

❸❸

Place
du Jeu
de Balle

Palais
de Justice

Place
Lôuise

Rue des
Quatre Bras

Av. Rue de Suède

Rue de Hollande

Rue d'Angleterre

Rue Féron

MAROLLES

Rue Pieremans

Rue Haute

Rue de Montserrat

Rue aux Laines

Rue des Wynants

Place
Bara

Rue Joseph Claes

Rue Émile Fontainas

Rue Fontainas

Porte de Hal

Porte De Hal

Av. Henri Jaspar

Hôtel Des Monnaies

Bd. de Waterloo

Av. de la Toison d'Or

Rue de l'Hôtel
des Monnaies

Rue Bosquet

Rue Jourdan

Rue de
Suisse

Rue Coenraets

❸❹

Rue Berckmans

Previous page: dépôt-Design.

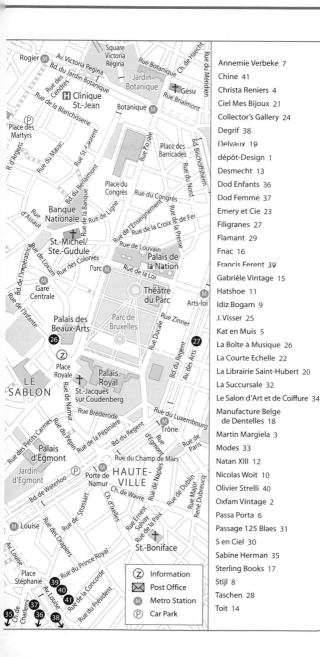

Ⓩ Information

✉ Post Office

Ⓜ Metro Station

Ⓟ Car Park

Shopping Best Bets

Best **Fabulous Accessories**
★★★ Natan XIII, *101 rue Antoine Dansaert (p 87)*

Best **Belgian Designer Names**
★★★ Stijl, *74 rue Antoine Dansaert (p 89)*

Best **Bargain Designer Clothes**
★★ Dod Femme, *64 rue du Bailli (p 90)*

Best **Antiques & Collectibles**
★ Passage 125 Blaes, *125 rue Blaes (p 87)*

Best **Real Belgian Lace**
★★ Manufacture Belge de Dentelles, *6–8 galerie de la Reine (p 92)*

Best **Classical Music**
★★ La Boîte à Musique, *74 Coudenberg (p 92)*

Best for **Literary Children**
★★ Passa Porta, *46 rue Antoine Dansaert (p 88)*

Best for **Beer Drinkers**
★ Beer Mania, *174–178 chaussée de Wavres (p 42)*

Relax at bookshop Passa Porta.

Best **Cutting-Edge Fashion**
★★ Martin Margiela, *114 rue de Flandre (p 89)*

Best **1950s' Jewelry**
★★ Collector's Gallery, *17 rue Lebeau (p 91)*

Best **Kitchenware**
★ Dille & Kamille, *16 rue Jean Stas (p 39)*

Best **Chocolatier**
★★★ Pierre Marcolini, *1 rue des Minimes (p 38)*

Best **Cookies**
★★ Dandoy, *31 rue au Beurre (p 37)*

Best **Discount Furniture & Homewares**
★★ dépôt-Design, *19 quai du Hainaut (p 90)*

Best **Vintage Clothing**
★★★ Modes, *164 rue Blaes (p 92)*

Best **Herbal Remedies**
★★ Desmecht, *10 place Sainte-Catherine (p 90)*

Best **Leather Goods**
★★★ Delvaux, *31 galerie de la Reine (p 87)*

Best for **Toys**
★ La Courte Echelle, *12 rue des Eponniers (p 89);* and Musée du Jouet, *24 rue de l'Association (p 51)*

Best **Children's Clothes**
★★ Kat en Muis, *32 rue Antoine Dansaert (p 89)*

Best **Contemporary Jewelry**
★★★ Sabine Herman, *86 rue Faider (p 91)*

Best for **Cartoons**
★ La Boutique Tintin, *13 rue de la Colline;* and ★★★ Centre Belge de la Bande Dessinée, *20 rue des Sables (p 46)*

Brussels **Shopping A to Z**

Delvaux for luxurious handmade bags.

Accessories

★★★ Delvaux GRAND' PLACE

This famous Brussels company has been hand-making the best and most expensive handbags and leather goods in Belgium since 1829. *31 galerie de la Reine.* ☎ *02 512 71 98. www.delvaux.com. AE, DC, MC, V. Métro: Gare Centrale or Bourse. Map p 84.*

★ Hatshoe ST.-GERY-DANSAERT

This tiny store stocks the best designer shoes for men and women from names such as Dries Van Noten, Nathalie Verlinden, and Marc Jacobs. *89 rue Antoine Dansaert.* ☎ *02 512 41 52. AE, DC, MC, V. Métro: Bourse. Map p 84.*

★★★ Natan XIII ST.-GERY-DAN-

SAERT Clothing label Natan has branched out into accessories. Its chic store stocks stunning bags and jewelry, by both known and unknown international names. *101 rue Antoine Dansaert.*

☎ *02 514 15 17. AE, DC, MC, V. Métro: Ste.-Catherine. Map p 84.*

★★★ S en Ciel

MAROLLES Expensive, beautifully handmade leather accessories attract the good citizens of Brussels to this wood-paneled, 100-year-old store located, surprisingly, in Marolles. This is the place to find a handbag, belt, or purse in perfectly cured, vibrantly colored leather and make a discrete, luxury statement. *158 rue Haute.* ☎ *02 511 77 46. www.s-en-ciel.be. AE, DC, MC, V. Bus: 27, 48. Map p 84.*

Antiques

★ La Succursale MAROLLES

This small store has an interesting, frequently changing selection of paintings and graphics, which the knowledgeable owners always research impeccably. *135A rue Blaes.* ☎ *0474 26 22 88. MC, V. Bus: 27 or 48 to Chapelle. Map p 84.*

★ Passage 125 Blaes

MAROLLES Thirty antique dealers on three floors offer a hotchpotch of items from the 18th century to the 1970s. There's everything here from lamps to cupboards, from Art Deco to retro. *125 rue Blaes.* ☎ *02 503 10 27. AE, MC. V. Bus: 27 or 48 to Chapelle. Map p 84.*

Art Galleries

★★★ J. Visser SABLON Brussels

is the European center for African art, so take advantage when you're here. This respected tribal art and antique specialist stocks sculpture, carvings, textiles, and jewelry from the whole of Africa. *37 rue Lebeau.* ☎ *02 503 49 42. www.tribal-art-visser.com. AE, MC. V. Bus: 48 to Grand Sablon. Map p 84.*

Antiques

Brussels sets great store by its antique shops, which are scattered across the city. Many of the top range stores are around the Place du Grand Sablon (catch the weekend antiques market Sat 9am–6pm; Sun 9am–2pm in front of the church). The lower end of the antiques market, verging into bric-a-brac, is in Marolles, along Rue Haute and Rue Blaes. The Place du Jeu de Balle has a daily flea market (7am–2pm), which is bigger at weekends.

★★ **Le Salon d'Art et de Coiffure** ST.-GILLES   Only in Brussels would you find a hairdressing salon that doubles as an art gallery and publishing house (*Editions La Pierre d'Alun*). *81 rue de l'Hôtel des Monnaies.* ☎ *02 537 65 40. No credit cards. Métro: Parvis de St.-Gilles. Map p 84.*

Books

★ **kids Filigranes** MADOU   One of the biggest French-language bookshops in Brussels with 120,000 titles. It's family friendly, with a children's storyteller on Sundays, and coffee and wine for magazine readers. *39–40 avenue des Arts.* ☎ *02 511 90 15. www.filigranes.be. AE, DC, MC, V. Métro: Arts-Loi. Map p 84.*

La Librairie Saint-Hubert.

★ **La Librairie Saint-Hubert** GRAND' PLACE   This elegant store specializes in books on fine art, architecture, photography, and travel. *2 galerie du Roi.* ☎ *02 511 24 12. www.librairie-saint-hubert. com. AE, DC, MC, V. Métro: Gare Centrale or Bourse. Map p 84.*

★★ **kids Passa Porta** ST.-GERY-DANSAERT   Opened in 2004, this international bookshop has comfortable chairs and a good range of titles in various languages. It also has a children's corner with comics, and hosts author evenings. *46 rue Antoine Dansaert.* ☎ *02 502 94 60. www.passaportabookshop.be. AE, DC, MC, V. Métro: Bourse. Map p 84.*

★ **Sterling Books** DE BROUCKÈRE   Brussels' largest English-language bookshop has over 50,000 British and American titles at reduced prices, fiction and non-fiction, newspapers, magazines, and stationery. *38 rue du Fossé aux Loups.* ☎ *02 223 62 23. www.sterlingbooks.be. AE, DC, MC, V. Métro: De Brouckère. Map p 84.*

★★ **Taschen** ST.-GILLES   The Philippe Starck-designed interior sets a chic note for a store owned and run by the ever expanding, top German publishing house of Taschen: Superb stock of art books and photographs. *16 rue Lebeau.* ☎ *02 513 80 23. www.taschen.com. Bus: 48, 95. Map p 84.*

Children's Toys & Clothes

★ kids **Kat en Muis** ST.-GERY-DANSAERT   Belgians spend a lot on children's clothes, and so for that special look, kit yours out here. *32 rue Antoine Dansaert.* ☎ *02 514 32 34. AE, DC, MC, V. Métro: Bourse. Map p 84.*

★ kids **La Courte Echelle** GRAND' PLACE   Enthusiasts come here for the dolls' houses and furniture from both big manufacturers and artists who still hand-make miniature household items. *12 rue des Eponniers.* ☎ *02 512 47 59. www. lacourteechelle.com. AE, DC, MC, V. Métro: Gare Centrale. Map p 84.*

Comics

Brussels is as famous for its comic tradition as for its chocolatiers. See Chapter 2, 'The Ninth Art—Cartoons,' p 44.

Designer Clothes

★★ **Annemie Verbeke** ST.-GERY-DANSAERT   Annemie started out as one of the famous Antwerp designers, but opened her own store in Brussels in 1999. Look for her asymmetric skirts and comfortably cut trousers in gentle rose, deep blues, and strong greens. *64 rue Antoine Dansaert.* ☎ *02 511 21 71. www.anne mieverbeke.be. AE, DC, MC, V. Métro: Bourse or Ste.-Catherine. Map p 84.*

★ **Chine** LOUISE   Belgian designer Guillaume Thys is known for his fashionable, colorful women's clothes inspired by soft lines and made from delicate fabrics from the Far East. *82–84 avenue Louise.* ☎ *02 512 45 52. www.chinecollection.com. AE, DC, MC, V. Métro: Louise. Map p 84.*

★★ kids **Francis Ferent** LOUISE   The flagship store for this chic boutique chain stocks international labels for men, women, and children from DKNY to Prada. *60 avenue Louise.* ☎ *02 545 78 30. www.ferent.be.*

AE, DC, MC, V. Métro: Louise. Map p 84.

★★ **Martin Margiela** ST.-GERY-DANSAERT   This Flemish-born designer's time with Jean-Paul Gaultier shows. The all-white store stocks haute couture with an edge. His use of different materials like ski gloves, playing cards, and old wigs has influenced major designers like Mark Jacobs. *114 rue de Flandre.* ☎ *02 223 75 20. www.maisonmartin margiela.com. AE, DC, MC, V. Métro: Ste.-Catherine or Bourse. Map p 84.*

★★ **Nicolas Woit** ST.-GERY-DANSAERT   The Belgian designer financed the store by selling his vintage Barbie collection. Clothes display his love of a more leisured, tailored time. Unusual fabrics fit perfectly with the current vogue for vintage threads. *80 rue Antoine Dansaert.* ☎ *02 503 48 32. www.nicolas woit.com. AE, DC, MC, V. Métro: Bourse or Ste.-Catherine. Map p 84.*

★★★ **Olivier Strelli** LOUISE   He's been likened to Calvin Klein and Armani for his contemporary classic approach, producing colorful clothes in glamorous and wearable styles. Produces clothes for men and women, handbags, shoes, and watches. *72 avenue Louise.* ☎ *02 512 56 07. www.strelli.be. AE, DC, MC, V. Métro: Louise. Map p 84.*

★★★ **Stijl** ST.-GERY-DANSAERT   Owner Sonia Noel first championed the names who are now Belgian's top designers for men and women: Ann Demeulemeester, Dries van Noten, Christian Wijnants, and Martin Margiela. *74 rue Antoine Dansaert.* ☎ *02 512 03 13. AE, DC, MC, V. Métro: Bourse. Map p 84.*

Discount Fashion

★ **Degrif** IXELLES   It may take you some time, but you can find top names in the international shoe world here, from Prada to Tod. Be warned, no exchanges or refunds. *47–49 rue Simonis.* ☎ *02 537 53 04, No credit cards. Bus: 54 to Trinité. Map p 84.*

★★ kids **Dod Enfants** IXELLES
Rummage with other mums for mostly French-designed creations for your young stars: Great prices, real bargains, and some real designer mistakes. Check the website for more locations. *8 rue du Bailli.* ☎ *02 640 60 40. www.dod.be. AE, DC, MC, V. Tram: 81, 94. Map p 84.*

★★ **Dod Femme** MADOU   Like all discount shopping, you take pot luck hunting for great bargains on designer clothes, mid-market names, and accessories. Expect the likes of Cardin, Calvin Klein, and Dolce & Gabbana all at least 50% off. Check the website for other locations. *44 chaussée de Louvain.* ☎ *02 218 24 68. www.dod.be. AE, DC, MC, V. Métro: Madou. Map p 84.*

Herbalist
★★ **Desmecht** ST.-GERY-DAN-SAERT   A dream of a traditional herbalist's shop, complete with intriguing wooden cabinets, dispensing tisanes, herbal remedies, consultations, and well-being since 1840 and from knowledgeable staff. *10 place Sainte-Catherine.* ☎ *02 511 29 59. www.desmecht.com. Métro: Ste.-Catherine. Map p 84.*

dépôt-Design for homeware bargains.

Household & Homeware
★★ **dépôt-Design** ANDERLECHT
Head over the canal to this vast warehouse for its range of end-of-line homeware and new stock. It's a pile-them-high, sell-them-(fairly)-cheap kind of store, though of a very superior kind, and prices are good. *19 quai du Hainaut.* ☎ *02 502 28 82. www.depotdesign.be. AE, DC, MC, V. Métro: Comte de Flandre. Map p 84.*

★★ **Emery et Cie** SABLON
Three floors in an old building are full of the kind of chic furniture that everyone loves, from wrought-iron

Department Stores & Galleries

Inno (www.inno.be) is the best-known department store with several Brussels branches. The most conveniently located are at 111 rue Neuve and 12 avenue Louise. Apart from the upscale **Galeries Royales de St.-Hubert** (p 9, ❹), check out the **Galerie de la Toison d'Or** on Avenue de la Toison d'Or and Chaussée d'Ixelles and its neighbor **Galerie Louise,** Avenue de la Toison d'Or and Avenue Louise. Both are at the upper end of the retail spectrum, with unique stores and top-name chains.

banquettes to terracotta bowls, richly colored throws, and glazed pots. *27 rue de l'Hôpital.* ☎ *02 513 58 92. www.emeryetcie.com. AE, DC, MC, V. Bus: 48, 95 to Saint-Jean. Map p 84.*

★★ **Flamant** SABLON One of Princess Mathilda's favorite addresses, this posh, pricey store displays its desirable objects in room settings: From large pieces of furniture to home accessories. *36 place du Grand-Sablon.* ☎ *02 514 47 07. www.flamant.com. AE, DC, MC, V. Bus: 48 to Grand Sablon. Map p 84.*

★ **Toit** ST.-GERY-DANSAERT This boutique-cum-gallery stocks crazy lamps alongside furnishing fabrics from Turkey to Senegal—old kilims, Chinese table sets, linen, pajamas, and more, all at reasonable prices. *46 rue des Chartreux.* ☎ *02 503 33 38. www.toit-bruxelles.be. AE, DC, MC, V. Métro: Bourse. Map p 84.*

Jewelry
★★ **Christa Reniers** ST.-GERY-DANSAERT This self-taught jeweler is one of Belgium's most famous designers, known for her bold,

contemporary shapes. Well worth a visit to her new premises. *196 rue Antoine Dansaert.* ☎ *02 510 06 60. www.christareniers.com. AE, DC, MC, V. Métro: Bourse. Map p 84.*

★★★ **Ciel Mes Bijoux** GRAND' PLACE For more than 20 years, Patrick and Godelive Sigal have been selling fabulous vintage jewelry from grand names such as Chanel, Balenciaga, and Dior. They also stock contemporary designers. *16 galerie du Roi.* ☎ *02 514 71 98. www.cielmes bijoux.com. AE, DC, MC, V. Métro: Gare Centrale. Map p 84.*

★★ **Collector's Gallery** SABLON Betty de Stefano sells vintage jewelry, mainly from the 1920s to the 1950s, but is also known for her Georg Jensen stock and contemporary jewelers such as Daniel von Weinberger. *17 rue Lebeau.* ☎ *02 511 46 13. www.collectors-gallery. com. AE, DC, MC, V. Bus: 48 to Grand Sablon. Map p 84.*

★★★ **Sabine Herman** IXELLES The eponymous jeweler trained in Antwerp opened here to sell her own precious, exquisitely designed,

Ciel Mes Bijoux.

handmade jewelry, and to promote other makers. The diverse mix takes in jewelry made of paper, wood, silver, silicon, precious stones, and gold with a price range for all. *86 rue Faider.* ☎ *02 640 72 53. www. sabineherman.be. AE, DC, MC, V. Tram: 81, 94. Map p 84.*

Lace

★★ **Manufacture Belge de Dentelles** GRAND' PLACE   This store has been providing wedding veils and baptism robes since 1810. According to your budget, go for real handmade lace with delicate patterns, or partially handmade items. *6–8 galerie de la Reine.* ☎ *02 511 44 77. www.mbd.be. AE, DC, MC. V. Métro: Gare Centrale or Bourse. Map p 84.*

Music

★ **Fnac** ROGIER   One of Europe's giant chains, this stocks a wide selection of CDs as well as MP3 players, DVDs, books, and newspapers. It also sells tickets to mainstream concerts and gigs. *City 2, Rue Neuve.* ☎ *02 275 11 11. www.fnac.be. AE, DC, MC, V. Métro: Roger. Map p 84.*

★★ **La Boîte à Musique** GARE CENTRALE   The biggest classical music store in Europe stocks more than 30,000 CDs and is allied to the independent classical record label Pavane Records. Its website will source any classical CD you want. *74 Coudenberg.* ☎ *02 513 09 65. www.classicalmusic.be. AE, DC, MC, V. Métro: Gare Centrale. Map p 84.*

Vintage Clothing

★★ **Gabrièle Vintage** ST.-GERY-DANSAERT   Gabrièle Wolf stocks clothes and accessories from the 1920s to the 1980s, chosen for their beauty and wearability rather than their haute couture labels. *27 rue des Chartreux.* ☎ *02 512 67 43. www.*

Gabrièle Vintage.

gabriele-wolf.neopathes.com. AE, DC, MC. V. Métro: Bourse. Map p 84.

★★ **Idiz Bogam** ST.-GERY-DAN-SAERT   You can buy quirky, individual secondhand and vintage ware from London, New York, and Paris in this unusual store: Also known for its vintage shoes (men's and women's). *76 rue Antoine Dansaert.* ☎ *02 512 10 32. AE, DC, MC, V. Métro: Bourse. Map p 84.*

★★★ **Modes** MAROLLES   One of Brussels' most serious vintage clothing stores, this specializes in pre-1950 and turn-of-the-century clothes and accessories. Museum curators, designers, and collectors come here for the coats, dresses, glasses, gloves, purses, and accessories that turn the place into a period film set. *164 rue Blaes.* ☎ *02 512 49 07. AE, MC, V. Bus: 48 to Chapelle. Map p 84.*

★★ **Oxfam Vintage** ST.-GERY-DANSAERT   Oxfam provides young designers with old materials that they make up into one-off clothes: Imaginative dresses, shirts, coats, and skirts to get you noticed at great prices. *104 rue de Flandre.* ☎ *02 522 40 70. Métro: Comte de Flandre. Map p 84.* ●

Bois de la Cambre

1 Etangs d'Ixelles
2 Abbaye de la Cambre
3 Bois de la Cambre
4 The Wood
5 Provelo
6 Le Chalet Robinson

When I first came to Brussels I expected a thoroughly urban city, with window boxes providing the only green touch. How delightfully wrong I was. Brussels is in fact one of Europe's greenest cities, with the southern corner merging into the vast Forêt de Soignes. For a taster, start at the delightful Bois de la Cambre. START: **Bus 71, 81 to Flagey.**

1 **Etangs d'Ixelles.** One thing I love about Brussels is the residential areas clustered quietly around peaceful parks and gardens. The ponds of the Etangs d'Ixelles, complete with plumes of water shooting skyward, are full of ducks in summer. Sought-after Art Nouveau buildings look out over the view from Rue de la Vallée (no. 40), Rue Vilain XIV (nos. 42 and 46), and Rue du Monastère. ⏱ *30 min.*

2 ★★ **Abbaye de la Cambre.** From the ponds, it's a short stroll

Previous page: Parc Léopold.

south to one of the most surprising corners of Brussels. The Abbey was founded in 1201 by the Cistercians and was finally closed by the invading French Revolutionary Army in 1796. All that's left is the church and its 14th-century cloister, surrounded by picturesque 18th-century buildings that today house the La Cambre art school and National Geographical Institute. It may sound clichéd, but with its formal gardens, the Abbey really does possess an astonishing tranquility. The only thing missing (surprisingly as we're in Brussels) is a good cafe. ⏱ *1 hr. Rue du Monastère.* ☎ *02 648 11 21. Free admission. Church Mon–Fri 9am–noon & 3–6pm; Sat 8am–12:30pm & 3–6pm; Sun 9am–12:30pm. Tram: 94 to Abbaye.*

③ ★★ kids Bois de la Cambre. Go a little farther south to the 120-hectare (297-acre) park that was formed out of the Forêt de Soignes. When this public park, with an artificial lake and crisscrossed with paths and roads, emerged after 6 years of work in 1868, it instantly became known as the Central Park of Brussels. Today it's full of walkers with their dogs, plus families, joggers, and bicyclists. ⏱ *1–2 hr.*

④ ★ kids The Wood. In summer, the terrace of this new bar/restaurant fills up, particularly for Sunday brunch. It's a great place for a meal or an exotic cocktail. Though relatively pricey, most people agree it's worth the extra for the view of the park. *3–4 avenue de Flore.* ☎ *02 640 19 68. www.thewood.be. $$$.*

⑤ ★ kids Provelo. On Sundays, Provelo hires out bicycles so you can take to the wooded paths with the wind in your face and the sound of birdsong ringing in your ears. Adult bikes from 4€ an hour to 13€ a day, children from 3€ to 12€. Check the website for more details. *Carrefour des Atelages. www. provelo.be.*

⑥ ★ kids Le Chalet Robinson. The original Chalet was built in 1877, burnt down twice, and has now re-emerged in all its Swiss-style glory in the middle of the lake. You get to it on a tiny ferry that plies back and forth, scattering the swans in its wake. The restaurant is delightful, serving everything from crepes, waffles, and tartines (open sandwiches), to serious meals of grilled tuna and steaks. *1 sentier de l'Embarcadère.* ☎ *02 372 92 92. www.chaletrobinson.be. $$.*

Abbaye de la Cambre.

Forêt de Soignes

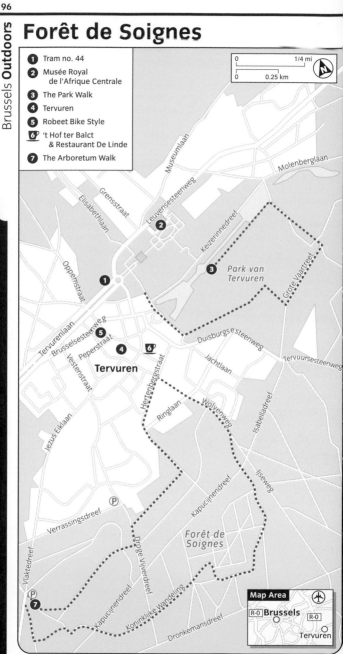

1. Tram no. 44
2. Musée Royal de l'Afrique Centrale
3. The Park Walk
4. Tervuren
5. Robeet Bike Style
6. 't Hof ter Balct & Restaurant De Linde
7. The Arboretum Walk

Map Area

Brussels

Tervuren

This walk is in two parts. The first walk is around 6km (4 miles), the second Arboretum walk is 7km (4½ miles). If you prefer to bicycle, hire one in Tervuren (see ❹). All the paths are well signposted, but if you get lost, ask anyone for directions. Aim to eat in Tervuren or take a picnic. START: **Métro to Montgomery.**

❶ ★★ kids **Tram no. 44.** Take tram 44 from Montgomery, which winds its way through the wealthy suburb of Woluwe Saint-Pierre. The route also passes the fabulous **Palais Stoclet,** a private house built by Josef Hoffman between 1905 and 1911. Still occupied by the family, it's being restored and currently not open to the public. ⏲ *30 min.*

❷ ★★ kids **Musée Royal de l'Afrique Centrale.** If you have time, dive into this huge, splendid museum. Opened in 1910, it was intended to show the world the riches accumulated—in the rather dubious ways of the 19th century—in Belgium's colonies, particularly the Congo. I love its old-fashioned feel and its very strong sense of 19th-century colonialism, though the whiff of paternalism lingers. There's a small but very good cafe. ⏲ *2 hr. See p 24, ❼.*

❸ ★★ kids **The Park Walk.** Formal French gardens, planted in 1897 for the Colonial Exhibition, stretch out from the back of the museum. Walk down and turn left onto Spaans-Huisdreef for a spectacular stroll beside the water. Continue to the 17th-century Goordaal mill, which is being restored, to the biggest lake in the park, surrounded by walnut, pine, maple, red beech, yellow dogwood, and more. Originally part of the Saint Gertrud Abbey in Louvain, the park here is thick with hornbeam, willow, poplar, and alder, and unusual plants like reed, cleavers, coltsfoot, mugwort, thistles, and herb-Robert. Turn right toward the Zevenster where several lanes meet. There are always children clambering on the three megaliths, popularly called 'druid stones,' and put here in 1902. The signposted path to Tervuren takes you onto Wildezwijenweg, to the monumental arched gate leading into the town. ⏲ *1½ hr.*

Musée Royal de l'Afrique Centrale.

The Forêt de Soignes

Reputedly the largest beech forest in Europe, this wonderfully wild 4,000 hectares (9,884 acres) is close to central Brussels, yet totally rural. Originally part of the huge Roman Forest of Ardennes, it was too rich a source to escape the needs of successive rulers. Napoleon cut down 22,000 oaks to build the fleet intended to attack England; the Duke of Wellington claimed parts around Waterloo and the family still gets income from it. The Bois de la Cambre was built from part of the forest in 1861. Once the habitat of bears and wolves, badgers, and hares, today there is still an abundance of wildlife including wild boars.

④ ★ kids **Tervuren.** This delightful small town dates back to the Middle Ages when its castle was a royal residence. But it was Léopold II who was the real benefactor of the town through his Royal Museum and connecting Tervuren to Brussels. There's a Tourist Office in the Markt, delightful old buildings, churches, and cafes. ⏱ *1–2 hr.*

⑤ ★★ kids **Robeet Bike Style.** If you haven't hired a bicycle in Brussels (p 168) you'll find one in Tervuren at very reasonable rates. *Brusselsesteenweg 72.* ☎ *02 767 43 38. www.robeet.be.*

⑥ ★ kids Grab a coffee and a snack in the cafes around the main square. Or try the cafe **'t Hof ter Balct** for a full meal: (30 Hoornzeelstraat. ☎ 02 768 24 60 $). In town **Restaurant De Linde** is a good bet. *Kerkstraat 8.* ☎ *02 767 87 42. www.delindetervuren.be. $$.*

⑦ ★★ kids **The Arboretum Walk.** If you're up to the additional 7km (4½ miles), walk through Tervuren along Jezus Eiklaan down to the arboretum's official entrance at Vlaktedreef. The 100-hectare (247-acre) Arboretum was laid out in 1902 by Léopold II. Organized geographically, there are more than 450 different species of tree. Follow the map and signposted paths through woods of Alaskan cypresses, towering Sequoias, monkey puzzle trees from the Chilean Andes, tall pines from the Mediterranean, and cedars from the Atlas Mountains. It's a magical experience and takes you far away from the hustle and bustle of Brussels. ●

Brussels **Dining**

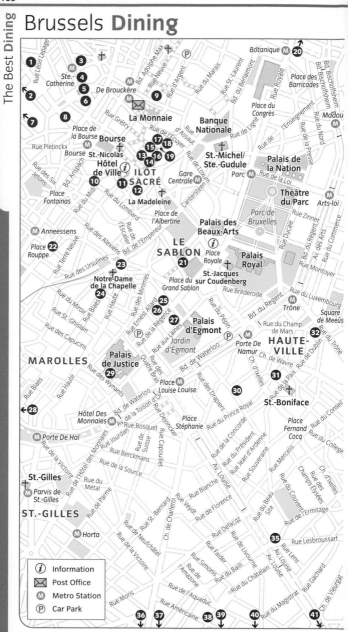

Legend:

- (i) Information
- ✉ Post Office
- Ⓜ Metro Station
- Ⓟ Car Park

Previous page: Cafe window displays, Brussels.

Arcadi **18**
Aux Armes de Bruxelles **13**
Belga Queen **9**
Bocconi **11**
Bon-Bon **36**
Bonsoir Clara **8**
Choz Léon **16**
Chou **32**
Comme Chez Soi **22**
François **6**
Jaloa **3**
L'Esprit de Sel **33**
L'Horloge du Sud **34**
L'Idiot du Village **24**
L'Ultime Atome **31**
La Clef des Champs **25**
La Manufacture **7**
La Quincaillerie **38**
La Roue d'Or **12**
La Taverne du Passage **17**
Le Café du Vaudeville **14**
Le Cercle des Voyageurs **10**
Le Chalet de la Forêt **41**
Le Fourneau **4**
Le Marmiton **19**
Le Pigeon Noir **37**
Les Brassins **30**
Les Brigittines aux Marchés
  de la Chapelle **23**
Les Dames Tartine **20**
Les Larmes du Tigre **29**
Lola **27**
Midi Station **28**
MuseumBrasserie **21**
Orphyse Chaussette **26**
Rouge Tomate **35**
Royal Brasserie Brussels **2**
Toucan sur Mer **40**
Vincent **15**
Vismet **5**
Viva M'Boma **1**
Winery **39**

The Best Dining

Dining Best Bets

Best Steak—Aux Armes de Bruxelles.

Best **Gourmet Restaurant**
★★★ Comme Chez Soi $$$$$ *23 place Rouppe (p 104)*

Best **Italian Food**
★★★ Bocconi $$$$ *1–3 rue de l'Amigo (p 103)*

Best for **Kids**
★ Chez Léon $$ *18 rue des Bouchers (p 104)*

Best for **Fashionistas**
★★ Belga Queen $$$$ *32 rue Fosse-aux-Loups (p 103)*

Best **Business Lunch**
★★ MuseumBrasserie $$$$ *Palais Royale des Beaux-Arts (p 109)*

Best **Value Neighborhood Restaurant**
★ Les Brassins $$ *36 rue Keyenveld (p 108)*

Best for **Modern Seafood**
★★ Vismet $$$ *32 place Sainte-Catherine (p 110)*

Best for **Sunny French Cooking**
★★ La Clef des Champs $$ *23 rue de Rollebeek (p 104)*

Best **Steak Around the Grand' Place**
★★ Aux Armes de Bruxelles $$$ *13 rue des Bouchers (p 103)*

Best for **Healthy Eaters**
★★ Rouge Tomate $$$ *190 avenue Louise (p 109)*

Best for **Gourmets in the Know**
★★★ Bon-Bon $$$ *93 rue des Carmelites (p 103)*

Best for **Something Offal**
★ Viva M'Boma $$ *17 rue de Flandre (p 110)*

Best for **Unusual Dishes**
★★ Le Café des Spores $$ *103 chaussée d'Alsemberg (p 39)*

Best for **Good Value**
★ Le Pigeon Noir $ *2 Geleytsbeek (p 107)*

Best for **the Freshest Seafood**
★★★ Toucan sur Mer $$$ *17–19 avenue Louis Lepoutre (p 109)*

Best **Thai Cooking**
★★ Les Larmes du Tigre $$ *21 rue Wynants (p 108)*

Best **Classic French**
★★★ Le Chalet de la Forêt $$$$$ *43 Drève de Lorraine (p 107)*

Best **Undiscovered Gem**
★★ Les Dames Tartine $$$ *58 chaussée de Haecht (p 108)*

Brussels **Dining A to Z**

Bocconi is one of the best restaurants in town.

kids Arcadi GRAND' PLACE *CAFE*
This simple cafe just by the Galeries
St.-Hubert serves quiches made
with imagination, plus sandwiches,
pastas, and good pastries and coffee. *1b rue d'Arenberg.* ☎ *02 511
33 43. Entrees 8.50€–12.90€. V.
Daily 7:30am–11pm. Métro: Gare
Centrale. Map p 100.*

★★ Aux Armes de Bruxelles
GRAND' PLACE *FRENCH/BELGIAN*
The traditional starched white linen
cloths and flambéed dishes were as
much loved by King Léopold III,
singer Jacques Brel, and tenor Plá-
cido Domingo as the enduring classics such as *waterzooi* (a creamy
stew), steak, and mussels. *13 rue
des Bouchers.* ☎ *02 511 55 50.
www.armesdebruxelles.be. Entrees
14.50€–24.50€; prix fixe 32€–
47.50€. AE, DC, MC, V. Daily noon–
11:15pm. Métro: Bourse. Map p 100.*

★★ Belga Queen DE BROUCKÈRE
MODERN FRENCH Achingly trendy,
innovatively designed—and that's
just the clientele. The menu promises
a bit more than it delivers, but you're
mainly here to see and be seen. *32
rue Fosse-aux-Loups.* ☎ *02 217 21 87.*

*www.belgaqueen.be. Entrees 20€–
45€; prix fixe during week 16€. AE,
DC, MC, V. Daily lunch & dinner.
Métro: De Brouckère. Map p 100.*

★★★ Bocconi GRAND' PLACE
ITALIAN Quite simply, this is the
best Italian restaurant in town,
located inside Brussels' top hotel.
Its relaxed atmosphere and sophisticated decor complements a menu
based on the freshest seasonal
ingredients, simply treated. *1–3 rue
de l'Amigo.* ☎ *02 547 47 15. www.
roccofortehotels.com. Entrees 26€–
35€; prix fixe 18€–34€ (lunch). AE,
DC, MC, V. Lunch & dinner daily.
Métro: Bourse. Map p 100.*

★★★ Bon-Bon ST. GILLES *FRENCH*
The chef Christophe Hardiquest is
one of Belgium's top young con-
tenders. The menu depends on the
market buys, and so expect inventive exciting cooking from the open
kitchen in a neighborhood location.
Take a 10-minute taxi ride out here
from the center. *93 rue des Carmel-
ites.* ☎ *02 346 66 15. Prix fixe 40€
(lunch); 67€–140€ (dinner). AE, DC,
MC, V. Lunch Tues–Fri; dinner Tues–
Sat. Tram: 92 to Leon. Map p 100.*

Modern European cuisine at Bonsoir Clara.

★★ **Bonsoir Clara** SAINT-GERY-DANSAERT *MODERN EUROPEAN* An integral part of the area's upwardly mobile trend, the bold, geometrically decorated walls, moody lighting, modern European flavors, and reasonable prices keep it packed. Dress up, not down. *22 rue Antoine Dansaert.* ☎ *02 502 09 90. www.bonsoirclara.be. Entrees 16€– 26€; prix fixe weekdays 14€. AE, DC, MC, V. Métro: Bourse. Map p 100.*

★ kids **Chez Léon** GRAND' PLACE *SEAFOOD* The same family have been delivering an enjoyable, inexpensive experience here since 1893. Don't expect gourmet food; sit inside for simple fare such as *moules et frites* (mussels and fries). *18 rue des Bouchers.* ☎ *02 511 14 15. www.chezleon.be. Entrees 9.38€–30.13€. AE, DC, MC, V. Daily noon–midnight. Métro: Bourse. Map p 100.*

★★ **Chou** HAUTE VILLE *SEAFOOD* Two rooms that combine old and new—the more spectacular one has a glass floor looking down at the cellar, wood paneling, and an open kitchen—Chou combines the feel of a bistro with some pretty nifty cooking. It's a popular choice with the E.U. bureaucrats who work locally. *4 place de Londres.* ☎ *02 511 92 38. www.restaurantchou.eu. Entrees*

27.50€–32.50€; prix fixe 45€. Mon–Fri lunch & dinner. AE, MC, V. Métro: Trône. Map p 100.

★★★ **Comme Chez Soi** CHAPELLE *CLASSIC FRENCH* Book weeks in advance for Brussels' top Michelin-rated restaurant. The Art Nouveau setting, classic French cooking, attentive service, and wide-ranging

Chez Léon.

wine list make a meal here a special occasion. *23 place Rouppe.* ☎ *02 512 29 21. www.commechezsoi.be. Entrees 31€–114€; prix-fixe lunch 55€, dinner 84€–191€. AE, DC, MC, V. Lunch Tues, Thurs–Sat; dinner Tues–Sat; closed mid-July–mid-Aug. Métro: Anneessens. Map p 100.*

★★ **François** SAINTE-CATHERINE *SEAFOOD* The same family still runs this popular, old-fashioned fish restaurant as when it opened in 1930. Lobster and oyster are the house specialties. *2 quai aux Briques.* ☎ *02 511 60 89. www. restaurantfrancois.be. Entrees 23€– 58€; prix fixe 25€ (lunch)–55€. AE, DC, MC, V. Lunch & dinner Tues–Sat. Métro: Sainte-Catherine. Map p 100.*

★★ **Jaloa** STE.-CATHERINE *BEL-GIAN* Ever since Jaloa opened in this former house of Vincent van Gogh, the locals have been beating a path to its door. A classic base with modern touches is evident in dishes such as crab with leek and apple, and *confit* (salted and slow-cooked) Wagyu beef. Chef Gaëtan Colin is a man to watch; he has plans for more restaurants. *5–7 place Ste.-Catherine.* ☎ *02 513 92 62. www.jaloa.com. Entrees 24€– 37€; prix fixe 22€ (lunch)–72€. AE, MC, V. Métro: Sainte-Catherine. Map p 100.*

★ **L'Esprit de Sel** CINQUANTE-NAIRE *BRASSERIE* Stop by for solid cooking of French and Belgian classics. Go for the rack of lamb or asparagus in season to play to the kitchen's strengths. *52–54 place Jourdan.* ☎ *02 230 60 40. www. espritdesel.be. Entrees 13.50€–23€; prix fixe 27€. AE, DC, MC, V. Lunch & dinner daily. Métro: Schuman. Map p 100.*

★ **kids L'Horloge du Sud** SAINT-BONIFACE *AFRICAN* Great cooking, using traditional ingredients such as plantain and the right

spices, good atmosphere, and impromptu African music make this a favorite for all-comers to this predominantly African suburb. *141 rue du Trône.* ☎ *02 512 18 64. www. horlogedusud.be. Entrees 9.50€– 14€; prix fixe 20€–27€. AE, DC, MC, V. Mon–Fri 11am–midnight, Sat 6pm–midnight. Métro: Trône. Map p 100.*

★★ **L'Idiot du Village** MAROLLES *BELGIAN* This brightly decorated eatery is as much fun as it sounds— a welcoming restaurant with sophisticated local cooking made from seasonal market ingredients. *19 rue Notre-Seigneur.* ☎ *02 502 55 82. Entrees 20€–30€. AE, DC, MC, V. Lunch & dinner Mon–Fri; closed mid-July–mid-Aug, Christmas–New Year. Bus: 27, 48 to Chapelle. Map p 100.*

★ **L'Ultime Atome** SAINT-BONI-FACE *BRASSERIE* This social center of the neighborhood has long hours, fine brasserie dishes, and slow service to suit the laid-back locals. *14 rue Saint-Boniface.* ☎ *02 513 48 84. www.ultime-atome.com. Entrees 14€–22€. AE, MC, V. Mon–Thurs 8:30am–12:30am; Fri & Sat 9am– 1:30am; Sun 10am–12:30am. Métro: Porte de Namur. Map p 100.*

★★ **La Clef des Champs** SABLON *FRENCH* There's a sunny feel in this small restaurant, which serves good French dishes such as pike perch with almonds, and guinea fowl with spices. *23 rue de Rollebeek.* ☎ *02 512 11 93. www. clefdeschamps.be. Entrees 19€– 23€; prix fixe 19€ (lunch Tues–Fri), 33.50€–44€. AE, MC, V. Tram: 92, 94 to Petit Sablon. Map p 100*

★ **La Manufacture** SAINTE-CATHERINE *FRENCH/INTERNA-TIONAL* The old industrial workshops of Delvaux have been turned into this large, fashionable restaurant with a huge terrace, which serves classic cooking with modern touches and attracts high-end diners. *12–20 rue Notre-Dame du Sommeil.* ☎ *02 502 25 25. www.manufacture.be. Entrees 14€–24.50€; prix fixe 14€ (lunch)–35.50€. AE, DC, MC, V. Lunch Mon–Fri, dinner Mon–Sat. Métro: Bourse. Map p 100.*

★ **kids La Quincaillerie** IXELLES *BELGIAN/FRENCH* This converted 1903 hardware shop is known for friendly service and robust food. Pavement tables are particularly popular. Look out for a chic clientele: French actors Catherine Deneuve and Alain Delon plus a whole crowd of Belgian celebs. *45 rue du Page.* ☎ *02 533 98 33. www.quincaillerie.be. Entrees 16.95€–46€; prix fixe 13€ (lunch)–25€. AE, DC, MC, V. Lunch Mon–Fri, dinner daily. Tram: 81 to Trinité. Map p 100.*

★ **La Roue d'Or** GRAND' PLACE *TRADITIONAL CAFE/BRASSERIE* It's all very turn-of-the-20th-century, with classic brasserie dishes, at this venerable cafe-restaurant that was a favorite with the Surrealists. *26 rue des Chapeliers.* ☎ *02 514 25 54. Entrees 15€–24€; prix fixe 12.50€. AE, DC, MC, V. Daily noon–midnight; closed mid-July–mid-Aug. Métro: Bourse. Map p 100.*

★ **La Taverne du Passage** GRAND' PLACE *BRASSERIE* Classic style reigns here, in the decor, avuncular waiters, traditional food, and clientele—a mix of smart locals and tourists after a piece of old-school Brussels. *30 galerie de la Reine.* ☎ *02 512 37 31. www.tavernedupassage.com. Entrees 14.90€–25.90€. AE, DC, MC, V. Daily noon–midnight; closed Jun; July Tues–Thurs. Métro: Gare Centrale. Map p 100.*

★ **Le Café du Vaudeville** GRAND' PLACE *BELGIAN/FRENCH* In the middle of the Galeries St.-Hubert, this cafe/bar/restaurant also has a beautiful little theater. The owners pride themselves on their huge choice of *gaufres* (waffles), both sweet and savory; otherwise go for classics such as hearty *carbonnades* (stews). *11 galerie de la Reine.* ☎ *02 511 23 45. www.cafeduvaudeville.be. Entrees 13€–24€; prix fixe lunch 12.50€. AE, MC, V. Mon–Sat 9am–midnight; Sun 9am–8pm. Métro: Gare Centrale. Map p 100.*

Le Cercle des Voyageurs GRAND' PLACE *INTERNATIONAL* A meeting place for travelers, both those on real journeys and those of the mind. It's a club that anyone can join, with international food as

La Manufacture.

La Roue d'Or.

widely traveled as the concept. Expect events, readings, and meetings, too. *18 rue des Grands-Carmes.* ☎ *02 514 39 48. www.lecercledes voyageurs.com. Entrees 10.50€– 22€. MC, V. Mon, Wed, Thurs 11am– 11pm, Fri 11am–midnight, Sat noon–midnight, Sun noon–10pm; lunch & dinner daily except Tues. Métro: Bourse or Anneessens. Map p 100.*

★★★ **Le Chalet de la Forêt** UCCLE *CLASSIC FRENCH* Among Belgium's top restaurants, this verdant place for a special occasion serves French food impeccably sourced and cooked, with a heavyweight wine list to match. You might need to save up. *43 drève de Lorraine.* ☎ *02 374 54 16. www.le chaletdelaforet.be. Entrees 32.50€– 54€; prix.fixe lunch 34€, menu 85€. AE, DC, MC, V. Lunch & dinner Mon– Fri. Bus: 136, 137, 365 to Avenue Van Bever. Map 100.*

★★ **Le Fourneau** SAINTE-CATHE-RINE *BISTRO/SEAFOOD* This modern, smart restaurant is always packed with diners sitting on bar stools watching the kitchen prepare small dishes, tapas style, which you choose by price and weight. Fish is the strong suit. *8 place Sainte-Catherine.* ☎ *02 513 10 02. www. evanrestaurants.be. Tapas dishes 9€–20€. AE, DC, MC, V. Lunch & dinner Tues–Sat; closed July or Aug (phone for dates). Métro: Sainte-Catherine. Map p 100.*

★ **Le Marmiton** GRAND' PLACE *FRENCH/BELGIAN/BRASSERIE* Cozy and welcoming, this stalwart still delivers the goods in an area that has so many mediocre restaurants. Classics are offered with a modern flourish. *43 rue des Bouchers.* ☎ *02 511 79 10. www.lemarmiton.be. Entrees 15.95€–27.50€; prix fixe 18.95€–21.95€. AE, DC, MC, V. Daily lunch & dinner. Métro: Gare Centrale. Map p 100.*

★ kids **Le Pigeon Noir** UCCLE *BELGIAN* This family-owned and run bistro is for both locals and tourists who appreciate good honest cooking at good honest prices amid the feel of a neighborhood restaurant. *Geleytsbeek 2.* ☎ *02 375 23 74. www.lepigeonnoir.be. Entrees*

Typical Belgian Dishes

You should try at least some of the classics to get an idea of Belgian cooking, which runs from the rustic and rural to the most sophisticated cuisine in the world. *Moules et frites* (mussels and fries) come in huge quantities with different flavor twists. *Stoemp* is mashed potatoes and seasonal vegetables served with sausages and bacon. *Waterzooi* (which unfortunately translates as 'watery mess') is a stew cooked in a cream-based broth—and can be based on eels, fish, or chicken. *Carbonnade flamande* is that famous, sweet-tasting beef braised in beer. *Anguilles au vert* (eels in green sauce) can be sublime but is an acquired taste. Belgians are also fond of steak *à l'americaine* (raw minced steak with raw onion, capers, and egg).

16€–29€; prix fixe lunch 20€. Lunch & dinner Mon–Fri. AE, MC, V. Bus: 60 to Chenaie. Map p 100.

★ **kids Les Brassins** IXELLES *TRADITIONAL BELGIAN* This is not only a simple restaurant serving hearty portions of Belgian *carbonnades*, steak, and *stoemp* (mashed potatoes and vegetables), but also a neighborhood bar with local Lambic brews and strong Trappist ale. *36 rue Keyenveld.* ☎ *02 512 69 99. www.lesbrassins.be. Entrees 11.50€–20€; prix fixe 9€ & 13.50€. No credit cards. Lunch Mon–Fri, dinner Mon–Sat. Métro: Louise. Map p 100.*

★★ **Les Brigittines aux Marchés de la Chapelle** MAROLLES *BRASSERIE* Not a place for the delicate, but if you appreciate shin of veal, beef cheeks, and other uncompromising tastes, book ahead at this Art Nouveau gem. *5 place de la Chapelle.* ☎ *02 512 68 91. www.lesbrigittines.com. Entrees 14.50€–28.75€. AE, DC, MC, V. Lunch Mon–Fri, dinner Mon–Sat. Bus: 48 to Chapelle. Map p 100.*

★★ **Les Dames Tartine** SAINT-JOSSE-TEN-NOODE *FRENCH/BELGIAN* A real discovery with some of the

best classic cooking in town—at very reasonable prices. Try the pig's trotter with foie gras, fig, and spices, and wash it down with one of 300 impeccably chosen bottles of wine. *58 chaussée de Haecht.* ☎ *02 218 45 49. Entrees 17€–22€; prix fixe 19€–39€. AE, DC, MC, V. Lunch Tues–Fri, dinner Tues–Sat. Métro: Botanique. Map p 100.*

★★ **kids Les Larmes du Tigre** LOUISE *THAI* A passion for Thai cooking took hold of Brussels some 20 years ago when this restaurant behind the Palais de Justice began offering authentic dishes. Their Sunday buffet lunch is especially good. *21 rue Wynants.* ☎ *02 512 18 77. www.leslarmesdutigre.be. Entrees 12€–17€; prix fixe 11€–35€. AE, DC, MC, V. Lunch Tues–Fri & Sun; dinner daily. Métro: Louise. Map p 100.*

★★ **Lola** SABLON *BELGIAN/BRASSERIE* A real favorite with smart Brussels, the contemporary decor still keeps its fashionable edge after 10 years. The cooking is a mix of classic and modern, the place buzzes, the atmosphere is convivial. *33 place du Grand Sablon.* ☎ *02 514 24 60. www.restolola.be.*

Entrees 17€–32€. AE, DC, MC, V. Lunch & dinner daily. Bus: 27, 48 to Grand Sablon. Map p 100.

★★ kids Midi Station BRUSSELS MIDI STATION INTERNATIONAL

A huge space with restaurant, brasserie, cigar bar, and stage right by the station and Eurostar with achingly trendy design. Something for everyone, but on Sundays try the 45€ brunch—an endless buffet, including wine and live music. Place Victor Horta. ☎ 02 526 88 00. www.midistation.eu. Entrees 9€–33€; prix fixe 16€–20€ (lunch); Sun brunch 45€. AE, DC, MC, V. Daily 7am–midnight. Métro: Gare du Midi. Map p 100.

★★★ MuseumBrasserie

ROYALE MODERN BELGIAN Attached to the museum, with a clientele of business people, ladies-who-lunch, and museum-goers, this offers top-notch cooking supervised by Peter Goossens, whose Michelin-starred reputation was established at his restaurant, Hof van Cleve at Kruishouten. Book ahead. Musées Royales des Beaux Arts. ☎ 02 508 35 80. www.museumfood.be. Entrees 16€–27€; prix fixe 30€–36€. AE, DC, MC, V. Lunch & dinner Tues–Sun. Tram: 92, 94 to Royale. Map p 100.

★ Orphyse Chaussette SABLON

FRENCH Charming, small bistro in an old house where the chef-owner champions wine (there's a 300-strong list) and recipes from the southwest of France. Classics cooked with gusto. 5 rue Charles Hanssens. ☎ 02 502 75 81. Entrees 23€–26€. Lunch & dinner Tues–Sun. AE, MC, V. Tram: 92, 94 to Petit Sablon. Map p 100.

★★ Rouge Tomate LOUISE

MODERN FRENCH Contemporary cooking comes with style at this restaurant that keeps your health as much as your taste buds in mind. Dishes come with a nutritionist's blessing; flavors courtesy of a creative chef. 190 avenue Louise. ☎ 02 647 70 44. www.rougetomate. be. Entrees 18€–29€; prix fixe 15€–22€ (lunch). AE, DC, MC, V. Lunch Mon–Fri, dinner Mon–Sat. Tram: 54, 81 to Bailli. Map p 100.

★★ Royal Brasserie Brussels

DANSAERT BRASSERIE This ultra trendy brasserie shows the creeping gentrification of the area near the Brussels Canal. It's bustling, glitzy, and serves very good food—at decent prices. You must book evenings and weekends. 103 rue de Flandre. ☎ 02 217 85 00. www. royalbrasseriebrussels.be. Entrees 12.50€–22.50€. AE, DC, MC, V. Daily noon–11pm. Métro: Comte de Flandre. Map p 100.

★★★ Toucan sur Mer IXELLES

FISH/SEAFOOD Close by its parent, Toucan Brasserie, this bright, white, buzzing new restaurant has a tang of the sea. Chefs cook at the teppanyaki grill. There are a few meat dishes, but this is a temple to oysters and fish, with the freshest of

MuseumBrasserie.

Splendid ceramic murals in Vincent.

ingredients on view and platters designed to share. Chic, sophisticated, and fun; this is here to stay. *17–19 avenue Louis Lepoutre.* ☎ *02 340 07 40. www.toucanbrasserie. com. Entrees 12.50€–59€. AE, DC, MC, V. Lunch & dinner daily. Bus: 60 to Tenbosch. Map p 100.*

★ **Vincent** GRAND' PLACE *FRENCH/ BELGIAN* Great ambience is the trademark of this welcoming restaurant that boasts marvelous ceramic murals. Go nostalgic with Belgian specialties such as *cod meunière* in lemon parsley butter. *8–10 rue des Dominicains.* ☎ *02 511 23 03. www. restaurantvincent.com. Entrees 17€–60.50€. AE, DC, MC, V. Lunch & dinner daily. Métro: De Brouckère. Map 100.*

★★ **Vismet** SAINTE-CATHERINE *BRASSERIE* Chef Tom Decroos uses fish supplied by his father, a fisherman in Ostende, for some top-class cooking. With its red brick, contemporary decor, Vismet is giving old-style neighboring

restaurants plenty of competition. *23 place Sainte-Catherine.* ☎ *02 218 85 45. Entrees 24.50€–37.50€. AE, MC, V. Tues–Sat lunch & dinner; closed Aug. Métro: Sainte-Catherine. Map p 100.*

★ **Viva M'Boma** SAINTE-CATHERINE *BELGIAN* This characterful white-tiled tripe shop pairs its offal with *stoemp*; eels, brains, and *carbonnades* make interesting eating. *17 rue de Flandre.* ☎ *02 512 15 93. Entrees 12€–25€. AE, MC, V. Lunch & dinner Mon, Tues, Thurs–Sat. Métro: Sainte-Catherine. Map p 100.*

★ **Winery** IXELLES *BELGIAN* A shop, wine bar, and restaurant, Winery is smart and savvy. The decor is plain; there are bottles everywhere and the daily specials, as well as the famous charcuterie plates, are chalked up on a blackboard. *18 place G. Brugmann.* ☎ *02 345 47 17. www.wineryonline.be. Entrees 8€–11€. AE, MC, V. Mon–Sat 11am–10pm. Bus 60 to G. Brugmann. Map p 100.* ●

Brussels Nightlife

Previous page: Street scene at night, Brussels.

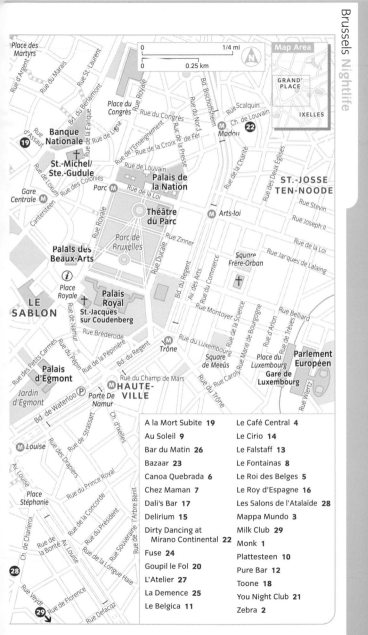

A la Mort Subite **19**	Le Café Central **4**
Au Soleil **9**	Le Cirio **14**
Bar du Matin **26**	Le Falstaff **13**
Bazaar **23**	Le Fontainas **8**
Canoa Quebrada **6**	Le Roi des Belges **5**
Chez Maman **7**	Le Roy d'Espagne **16**
Dali's Bar **17**	Les Salons de l'Atalaïde **28**
Delirium **15**	Mappa Mundo **3**
Dirty Dancing at	Milk Club **29**
Mirano Continental **22**	Monk **1**
Fuse **24**	Plattesteen **10**
Goupil le Fol **20**	Pure Bar **12**
L'Atelier **27**	Toone **18**
La Demence **25**	You Night Club **21**
Le Belgica **11**	Zebra **2**

Nightlife Best Bets

Experience a Jacques Brel moment at A la Mort Subite.

Best for Trendies
★★ Mappa Mundo, *2–6 rue du Pont de la Carpe (p 116)*

Best Bar on the Grand' Place
★★ Le Roy d'Espagne, *1 Grand' Place (p 116)*

Best for Singles
★ Le Cirio, *18–20 rue de la Bourse (p 115)*

Best for Patrick Swayze Fans
★★ Dirty Dancing at Mirano Continental, *38 chaussée de Louvain (p 117)*

Best for a Gay Sunday Afternoon Tea Dance
★★ You Night Club, *18 rue Duquesnoy (p 118)*

Best for a Jacques Brel Moment
★★ A la Mort Subite, *7 rue Montagne aux Herbes-Potagères (p 115)*

Best for a Drink with a King
★ Le Belgica, *32 rue du Marché au Charbon (p 118)*

Best for a Drink with a Queen
★ Chez Maman, *7 rue des Grands Carmes (p 118)*

Best for Couples over 30
★★ Les Salons de l'Atalaïde, *89 chaussée de Charleroi (p 116)*

Best for a Drunk Monk
★ A L'Imaige de Nostre-Dame, *Rue du Marché aux Herbes (p 42)*

Best for the Latest Techno Beats
★★ Fuse, *208 rue Blaes (p 117)*

Best for an Oxygen Rush
★ Pure Bar, *46 rue des Pierres (p 116)*

Best for Latin Lovers
★★ Canoa Quebrada, *53 rue du Marché au Charbon (p 117)*

Best for a Drink on the Terrace
★ Au Soleil, *86 rue du Marché au Charbon (p 115)*

Best for Dancing to the Beat
★★ Le Café Central, *14 rue Borgval (p 117)*

Brussels Nightlife A to Z

Bars & Wine Bars

★★★ A la Mort Subite GRAND' PLACE Casual passers-by might miss this bar on an untouristy street, but dedicated beer drinkers will have its address engraved on their hearts. It's legendary for the Art Nouveau architecture, for the name (meaning 'sudden death'), and for Jacques Brel, its most famous regular. *7 rue Montagne aux Herbes Potagères.* ☎ *02 513 13 18 www. alamortsubite.com. Métro: Gare Centrale. Map p 112.*

★ Au Soleil GRAND' PLACE This former gentlemen's outfitters—still with its original shop fittings—is a real Brussels *estaminet* (small cafe) with jazz music in the background, light snacks, and a terrace. *86 rue du Marché au Charbon.* ☎ *02 513 34 30. Métro: Bourse. Map p 112.*

★★ Bar du Matin ST.-GILLES Stylish and welcoming, this relatively new Art Deco-themed bar is far enough out of the center to avoid the crowds. Good for meeting friends, and with great varied live music and DJs. *172 chaussée d'Alsemberg.* ☎ *02 537 71 59. bardumatin.blogspot.com. Métro: Albert. Map p 112.*

★ Delirium GRAND' PLACE Down a narrow lane by the Grand' Place, this huge two-storey place (with terrace) has around 2,000 beers (go on, count them): Fun, noisy, and crowded with beer fans of all generations. A few steps along the alley takes you to Jeanneken-Pis, the tasteless female version of the jollier Manneken-Pis. *4A impasse de la Fidelité.* ☎ *02 514 44 34. www. deliriumcafe.be. Métro: Bourse. Map p 112.*

★★ Goupil le Fol GRAND' PLACE One of the most eccentric bars in Brussels, it's tiny and crowded with over-30s, stuffed full of clutter, including Jacques Brel memorabilia and an old jukebox that turns a night here soggy with nostalgia. *22 rue de la Violette.* ☎ *02 511 13 96. Métro: Gare Centrale. Map p 112.*

★ L'Atelier IXELLES A bit off the beaten track and near the university, this crowded bar posts its 200-strong beer menu on the walls. It's far enough out to be pretty free of tourists if you want some local atmosphere. *62 rue Elise.* ☎ *02 649 19 52. Tram: 94, bus 71 to Jeanne. Map p 112.*

★★ Le Cirio GRAND' PLACE I just sit here and sip my half-en-half (half-still, half-sparkling wine) and watch the world go by. It has an authentic Art Nouveau interior complete with old furnishings and fittings. *18 rue de la Bourse.* ☎ *02 512 13 95. Métro: Bourse. Map p 112.*

Le Cirio.

Le Falstaff GRAND' PLACE   Le Falstaff is probably the most famous bar in Brussels, but the atmosphere isn't helped by the scores of tourists. Despite this, it remains a genuine Brussels institution with a fabulous Art Nouveau interior. *19–25 rue Henri Maus.* ☎ *02 511 87 89. www.lefalstaff.be. Métro: Bourse. Map p 112.*

★★ **Le Roi des Belges** ST.-GERY-DANSAERT   Another immensely successful bar set up by the entrepreneur Fred Nicolay, this carries all his hallmarks: it's stylish, hip, minimalist, and serves great cocktails to trendy 20-somethings. *35 rue Jules van Praet.* ☎ *02 513 51 16. Métro: Bourse. Map p 112.*

★★ **Le Roy d'Espagne** GRAND' PLACE   Both restaurant and bar, this is a fabulous place for taking in the atmosphere of one of the most famous squares in the world. You'll have to fight for a table. *1 Grand' Place.* ☎ *02 513 08 07. www.roy despagne.be. Métro: Gare Centrale. Map p 112.*

★★ **Les Salons de l'Atalaïde** IXELLES   Renovated and re-opened, this restaurant and bar located inside an old house is as theatrical as ever. The decor mixes East and West, with armchairs and sofas to lie back in, and deadly cocktails. *89 chaussée de Charleroi.* ☎ *02 537 21 54. www.lessalonsatalaide.be. Métro: Porte de Hal. Map p 112.*

★★ **Mappa Mundo** ST.-GERY-DANSAERT   One of the first bars that set this area alight, it remains one of the most laid-back. It has a great terrace, upstairs rooms to relieve the crush, and a dangerous cocktail menu to see you through the night. *2–6 rue du Pont de la Carpe.* ☎ *02 514 35 55. Métro: Bourse. Map p 112.*

Try 'Sudden Death' beer at Monk, once known as A la Couronne.

★ **Monk** ST.-GERY-DANSAERT   This cavern of an old-fashioned bar with a wooden floor, tables, and chairs is always full of locals and tourists. There's a great beer list, including Mort Subite ('sudden death') for that end-of-my-life feeling. *42 rue Ste.-Catherine.* ☎ *02 503 08 80. www.monk.be. Métro: Bourse. Map p 112.*

★ **Pure Bar** GRAND' PLACE   After you've done the cocktail list, why not try a whiff of pure oxygen to recharge your batteries? Following that, try the shisha (Arabic water pipes to smoke). Or you could just take a fresh mint tea. *46 rue des Pierres.* ☎ *0473 48 55 45. www. pure-bar.be. Métro: Bourse. Map p 112.*

★★ **Toone** GRAND' PLACE   This place is as well known for its bar as for its puppet theater (p 126) and both are equally entertaining. Puppets hang from the ceiling and stand immobile in the old theater; wooden tables and chairs fill the rooms. *Impasse Ste.-Pétronile, 21 petite rue des Bouchers.* ☎ *02 513 54 86. www.toone.be. Métro: Bourse. Map p 112.*

★★ **Zebra** ST.-GERY-DANSAERT Industrial style for the younger generation rules here, in another of the cool bars that line the Place St.-Géry giving it such a vibe. Terrace heaters keep the drinkers warm outside pretty much whatever the weather. *33 place du St.-Géry.* ☎ *02 511 09 01. Métro: Bourse. Map p 112.*

Dance Clubs/Music Bars

★★ **Bazaar** MAROLLES The old warehouse comes alive at weekends when DJs spin disco, pop, and techno to a funky, well-dressed crowd. There's also a restaurant upstairs and a bar with (of all things) a hot air balloon. *63 rue des Capucins.* ☎ *02 511 26 00. www.bazaar resto.be. No cover charge. Bus: 27, 48 to Jeu de Balle. Map p 112.*

★★ **Canoa Quebrada** GRAND' PLACE Latino lovers flock to this heaving Brazilian place to salsa the night away while keeping fuelled up

Toone is also a popular puppet theater.

with plenty of adventurous cocktails. *53 rue du Marché-au-Charbon.* ☎ *02 502 83 30. www.canoa-quebrada.be. No cover charge. Métro: Bourse. Map p 112.*

★★ **Dali's Bar** GRAND' PLACE Sit in one of those famous sofas shaped like lips, sip a cocktail, and take in the atmosphere. That's before the house, reggae, and other music gets you going. From 10pm to late. *35 petite rue des Bouchers.* ☎ *02 511 54 67. No cover charge. Métro: Bourse. Map p 112.*

★★ **Dirty Dancing at Mirano Continental** ROYALE A mix of the casual and the designer-dressed frequent this former 1950s cinema, particularly for Saturday's Dirty Dancing nights when international DJs play house and garage from 11pm. *38 chaussée de Louvain.* ☎ *02 227 39 70. www.mirano.be. www.dirtydancing.be. Cover 10€. Métro: Louise. Map p 112.*

★★ **Fuse** MAROLLES This minimalist Marolles hotspot is *the* place to go wild to the techno and house beats. International DJs such as DEG and Pierre keep dancers up until 7am at weekends. *208 rue Blaes.* ☎ *02 511 97 89. www.fuse.be. Cover 5€ before midnight, 10€ after. Métro: Porte de Hal. Map p 112.*

★★ **Le Café Central** ST.-GERY-DANSAERT The famous old Acrobate became the Café Central; it's great for a young crowd who go for the concerts and the techno music pumped out by different DJs from Thursday to Saturday. Otherwise, join the older lot for Sunday screenings at 8pm of classic movies such as *Ivan the Terrible* and *Jules et Jim.* Dress retro. *14 rue Borgval.* ☎ *02 513 73 08. www.lecafecentral.com. Charges vary according to the night. Métro: Bourse. Map p 112.*

★ **Milk Club** LOUISE Top DJs are always on the menu at this small,

Stay up all night at Fuse.

laid-back place, spinning dance, garage, and electronic disco as well as house. Thursdays are for pop; Fridays and Saturdays it gets noisier with electro house and garage. *40 rue de Livourne.* ☎ *02 534 26 67. Cover 5€ after midnight. Métro: Louise. Map p 112.*

★★ **You Night Club** GRAND' PLACE   Designed by Miguel Cancio Martins (of Buddha Bar in Paris fame), You is big, brash, and psychedelic, with a designer clientele to match. Different themed music nights DJ'd by the likes of Milo culminate on Sunday with a popular tea dance for gays and lesbians, during the un-tea-like hours of 8pm to 2am. *18 rue Duquesnoy.* ☎ *02 639 14 00. www.leyou.be. Cover free–10€ (inc. drink(s)). Métro: Gare Centrale. Map p 112.*

Gay & Lesbian Bars/Clubs

★ **Chez Maman** GRAND' PLACE It may be tiny, but Chez Maman's an institution, mainly due to the owner 'Maman' and his fabulous transvestite shows. They flaunt it on the bar, growling out old songs on Fridays and Saturdays until dawn. *7 rue des Grands Carmes. No phone. www.chezmaman.be. No cover charge. Métro: Bourse. Map p 112.*

★★ **La Demence** MAROLLES Each month a huge gay evening for men only takes over Fuse (p 117). It's become an international event, and one of the hottest parties across gay Europe. *208 rue Blaes.* ☎ *02 511 97 89. www.lademence. com. Cover 15€–30€. Métro: Porte de Hal. Map p 112.*

★ **Le Belgica** GRAND' PLACE   A bar built as a dive—real or fake, it doesn't matter which. The clientele love what the two film-set designers did, right down to the bust of Léopold II on the bar. This famous pickup joint keeps moving from 10pm until 3am, Thursday to Sunday. *32 rue du Marché au Charbon.* ☎ *02 514 03 24. No cover charge. www. lebelgica.be. Métro: Bourse. Map p 112.*

★★ **Le Fontainas** GRAND' PLACE This small, friendly, and immensely popular bar and cafe is always busy, from coffee in the morning to the filled terrace on summer evenings when the music gets going. Near the St. Jacques gay district and always a large gay clientele in the evenings. *91 rue du Marché au Charbon.* ☎ *02 503 31 12. No cover charge. Métro: Annessens or Bourse. Map p 112.*

Plattesteen GRAND' PLACE   This traditional cafe–bar caters for all kinds, but its terrace in summer is the social center of Brussels' gay quarter. *41 rue du Marché au Charbon.* ☎ *02 512 82 03. No cover charge. Métro: Bourse. Map 112.* ●

8

The Best **Arts & Entertainment**

Brussels **Arts & Entertainment**

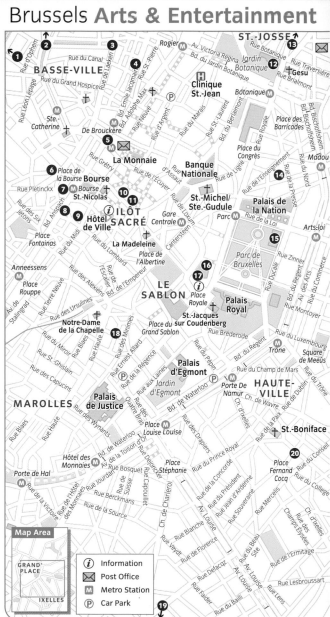

Previous page: Costume Festival, Brussels.

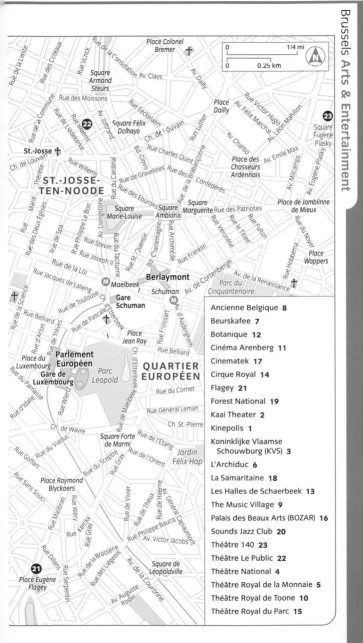

Ancienne Belgique **8**
Beurskafee **7**
Botanique **12**
Cinéma Arenberg **11**
Cinematek **17**
Cirque Royal **14**
Flagey **21**
Forest National **19**
Kaai Theater **2**
Kinepolis **1**
Koninklijke Vlaamse
   Schouwburg (KVS) **3**
L'Archiduc **6**
La Samaritaine **18**
Les Halles de Schaerbeek **13**
The Music Village **9**
Palais des Beaux Arts (BOZAR) **16**
Sounds Jazz Club **20**
Théâtre 140 **23**
Théâtre Le Public **22**
Théâtre National **4**
Théâtre Royal de la Monnaie **5**
Théâtre Royal de Toone **10**
Théâtre Royal du Parc **15**

Arts & Entertainment Best Bets

Best **Black-and-White Moment**
★★ Cinematek, *9 rue Baron Horta* (p 123)

Best **Place for Film Fans**
★ Flagey, *Place Sainte-Croix* (p 123)

Best for **Jazz in a New York-like Setting**
★★ The Music Village, *50 rue des Pierres* (p 126)

Best for **Opera Lovers**
★★ Théâtre Royal de la Monnaie, *Place de la Monnaie* (p 126)

Best **Theater for Kids**
★★ Théâtre Royal de Toone, *21 petite rue des Bouchers* (p 126)

Best **Local Jazz Night**
★★ Sounds Jazz Club, *28 rue de la Tulipe* (p 126)

Best **Contemporary Music Venue**
Kaai Theater, *20 place Sainctelette* (p 124)

Best **Place for Molière**
★ Théâtre Royal du Parc, *3 rue de la Loi* (p 125)

Best for **Belgium's National Orchestra**
★★★ Palais des Beaux Arts (BOZAR), *22 rue Ravenstein* (p 125)

Serious puppetry at Théâtre Royal de Toone.

Best for **Rock & Indie Gigs**
★★ Ancienne Belgique, *111 boulevard Anspach* (p 123)

Best **Long-Established Jazz Club**
★★★ L'Archiduc, *6 rue Antoine Dansaert* (p 126)

Best for **World Music**
★★ Les Halles de Schaerbeek, *22A rue Royale-Sainte-Marie* (p 124)

Buying Tickets

Listings of theater and dance, concerts, and films are published in the 'What's On' section of the weekly English-language *Bulletin Unlimited.* Tickets and schedules are available at the Tourist Office on Grand' Place (p 171) and at Fnac (p 92). Last-minute tickets up to 50% off are sold by **Arsene50** (www.arsene50.be). They have two locations: Cinéma Arenberg, 26 galerie de la Reine; and Flagey ticket office, Place Sainte-Croix; opening hours are Tuesday to Saturday 12:30pm to 5:30pm. You can also book theater, concerts, and sports online at www.onlineseats.com.

Arts & Entertainment A to Z

Cinema

★ Cinéma Arenberg GRAND' PLACE   This renovated Art Deco building houses a cinema known for arthouse and independent films. Foreign films are either dubbed or subtitled. *28 galerie de la Reine* ☎ *02 512 80 63. www.arenberg.be. Tickets: 8€. Métro: Gare Centrale. Map p 120.*

★★ Cinematek GRAND' PLACE Reopened in the Bozar complex after refurbishment, this is the place to see black-and-white silent movies with piano accompaniment, or today's cult offerings. A small exhibition shows how film was born, and you can access and watch old films on computers: Book in advance. *9 rue Baron Horta.* ☎ *02 551 19 19. www.cinematek.be. Tickets 3€. Métro: Gare Centrale. Map p 120.*

★ Flagey IXELLES   Flagey shows a wide range of films, in all languages, and showcases different international directors. It also hosts the **Brussels European Film Festival** in July every year. *Tickets 7€. See p 120.*

★★★ kids Kinepolis HEYSEL Twenty-five cinemas and one IMAX cinema make up this huge complex where all the major international films are shown—most in V.O. (*version originale*), i.e. English with French and Flemish subtitles. *20 boulevard du Centenaire, Bruparck.* ☎ *02 474 26 03. www.kinepolis.be. Tickets 7€–9€. Métro: Heysel. Map p 120.*

Concert & Rock Venues

★★ Ancienne Belgique GRAND' PLACE   Two different spaces offer serious enthusiasts great indie and rock bands. It's also the place to look out for new home-grown talent from jazz to contemporary. *110 boulevard Anspach.* ☎ *02 548 24 84. www.abconcerts.be. Tickets 12€– 50€. Métro: Bourse. Map p 120.*

★★ Botanique ROGIER   In the former glasshouses of the Jardin Botanique, the cultural center of the French-speaking community hosts concerts, exhibitions, films, and multicultural festivals. The festival, **Les Nuits Botaniques** in May features indie rock, French chansons, and rap—French style like you've not heard before. *236 rue Royale.* ☎ *02 218 37 32. www.botanique.be. Tickets 12€–19€. Métro: Botanique. Map p 120.*

★★ Forest National FOREST This is Brussels' big venue for top international names. Book way in advance for the likes of Spandau Ballet, The Cranberries, Jamie Cullum, Crowded House, and Riverdance. *208 avenue Victor Rousseau.* ☎ *from abroad: 70 25 20 20; in Belgium 0900 69 500. www.forest national.be. Tickets 29€–43€ Tram: 32, 82, 97 to Zaman. Map p 120.*

Dance, Music & Theater

★★★ Cirque Royal MADOU Built in 1879 as an indoor circus, this was transformed in 1953 into a multi-purpose hall for all kinds of spectacles. It has a name for booking indie rock and new-wave bands before they become famous. It puts on concerts, opera, dance, variety, review, folk, and rock music. *81 rue de l'Enseignement.* ☎ *02 218 20 15. www.cirque-royal.org. Tickets 22€– 65€. Métro: Madou. Map p 120.*

Festivals & Events

The Festival Ars Musica (www.arsmusica.be) in March brings top international musicians to venues such as Bozar (p 125). In April **Art Brussels** (www.artbrussels.be), a major contemporary arts fair, takes place at Brussels Expo, north of the city. The last weekend in May sees the **Brussels Jazz Marathon** (www.brusselsjazz marathon.be), with over a hundred free concerts in small and large venues, including open-air concerts in the Grand' Place. May also sees the **Queen Elisabeth International Music Competition** (www.cmireb.be), for young musicians. Grand' Place attracts beer devotees in early September with the annual **Beer Weekend** (www. weekenddelabiere.be). The **Skoda Jazz Festival** (www.skodajazz. be) takes place through October and November in various venues.

★★ **Flagey** IXELLES   The former home of Belgium's national radio, opened in 1938, Flagey is now a venue for modern, as well as classical, popular, and traditional music. From Catalan Music Days to the 2-day Jazz Marathon (see box, Festivals & Events), this is a seriously trendy venue. *Place Sainte-Croix.* ☎ *02 641 10 10. www.flagey.be. Tickets 5.50€– 37€. Bus: 71 to Flagey. Map p 120.*

★ **Kaai Theater** YSER   Known for concerts from 20th- and 21st-century

Multi-arts venue Flagey.

composers, this beautiful Art Deco theater also puts on dance and avant-garde plays, with some performances in English. *19 place Sainctelette.* ☎ *02 201 59 59. www. kaaitheater.be. Tickets 7.50€–25€. Métro: Yser. Map p 120.*

Koninklijke Vlaamse Schouwburg (KVS) SAINTE-CATHERINE
The Royal Flemish theater is known for its new experimental productions in Flemish as much as for its classics. If you don't speak Flemish, go for the exciting modern dance performances. *7 quai aux Pierres de Taille.* ☎ *02 210 11 00. www.kvs.be. Tickets 5€–20€. Métro: Yser. Map p 120.*

★★ **Les Halles de Schaerbeek** SCHAERBEEK   This magnificent iron-and- glass structure, one of the last great examples of 19th-century industrial architecture, is now a multimedia cultural center and one of the major venues in Brussels, even though it's outside the center. Programs range from hip-hop to world music, dance, theater, and theatrical happenings around a theme. *22A rue Royale-Sainte-Marie.* ☎ *02 218 21 07. www.halles.be. Tickets 5€–22€. Tram: 92, 94 to Sainte-Marie. Map p 120.*

The Horta-designed Palais des Beaux Arts.

★★★ Palais des Beaux Arts (BOZAR) ROYALE
This Horta-designed building houses Belgium's national orchestra (www.onb.be). The resident theater company, Le *Rideau de Bruxelles*, performs in French. You can also catch classical ballet and modern dance. The mix of programs and the emphasis on contemporary arts and controversial exhibitions make this one of the most dynamic venues in Brussels. *23 rue Ravenstein.* ☎ *02 507 82 00. www.bozar.be. Tickets 9€–50€. Métro: Gare Centrale. Map p 120.*

★ Théâtre 140 E.U. QUARTER
For more than 40 years, this place has had a reputation for avant-garde dance and performance from international names. *140 avenue E.-Plasky.* ☎ *02 733 97 08. www. theatre140.be. Tickets 15€–38€. Bus: 29, 63 to Plasky. Map p 120.*

★ Théâtre Le Public MADOU
This major French-speaking theater puts on a wide range of classics. *64–70 rue Braemt.* ☎ *0800 944 44. www.theatrelepublic.be. Tickets 22€. Métro Madou. Map p 120.*

★★ Théâtre National ROGIER
The national theater of the French-speaking part of Belgium opened in a new building in 2004. Performances range from classics to boulevard, opera, dance, and cabaret. *111–115 boulevard Emile Jacqmain.* ☎ *02 203 41 55. www.theatre national.be. Tickets 12€–22€. Métro: Rogier. Map p 120.*

★ Théâtre Royal du Parc ROYALE
This beautiful theater built in 1782 puts on both classic plays—from Molière to Brecht—and contemporary pieces, all in French. *3 rue de la Loi.* ☎ *02 505 30 40. www.theatre duparc.be. Tickets 5€–30€. Métro: Parc. Map p 120.*

Jazz Venues & Music Clubs

★ Beurskafee SAINT-GERY-DAN-SAERT
This Flemish multi-purpose venue housed in an 1885 building has different spaces for theater, music, and film, with mainly jazz played in the concert space. Friday and Saturday nights there's dancing to DJs in the club and the lounge. *22–28 rue Auguste-Orts.* ☎ *02 550 03 50. Tickets 12€. www.beursschouwburg.be. Métro: Bourse. Map p 120.*

For classic and contemporary French plays, visit the Théâtre Royal du Parc.

★★★ L'Archiduc SAINT-GERY-DANSAERT

It's been around since 1937 and if there's one jazz venue you visit in Brussels, it has to be L'Archiduc. Nat King Cole allegedly played here; today's jazz bands are also of a high caliber. There's live jazz on Sundays, music nightly, and the place is open from 4pm to 5am. *6 rue Antoine Dansaert.* ☎ *02 512 06 52. www.archiduc.net. No cover charge. Métro: Bourse. Map p 120.*

★ La Samaritaine SABLON

An atmospheric 17th-century cellar is the setting for an interesting range of music. One night it might be a jazz harpist, the next a solo singer. *16 rue de la Samaritaine.* ☎ *02 511 33 95. www.lasamaritaine.be. Cover 12€. Métro: Gare Centrale. Map p 120.*

★★ The Music Village GRAND' PLACE

I love this brick-walled, bar-cum-concert space where you sit packed together for good jazz from Wednesday to Saturday. All kinds are played, from Django Rheinhart's guitar jazz style to Cuban. *50 rue des Pierres.* ☎ *02 513 13 45. www.the musicvillage.com. Cover 7.50€–20€. Métro: De Brouckère. Map p 120.*

★ Sounds Jazz Club IXELLES

This well-established jazz club has jazz Monday to Saturday with music starting at 10pm. In the past it has hosted John Abercrombie and Aka Moon; today it presents the likes of Gerdband and the Salsa master Chamaquiando. *28 rue de la Tulipe.* ☎ *02 512 92 50. www.soundsjazz club.be. Cover from 7€. Bus: 54, 71 to Fernand Cocq. Map p 120.*

Opera

★★ Théâtre Royal de la Monnaie DE BROUCKERE

Belgium's main opera house is known for bold staging, a wide repertoire, and the new talent it encourages in its opera, dance, and concerts. The theater was rebuilt by Joseph Poelaert after a fire in 1856. In 1830, a particularly patriotic libretto in Auber's *The Mute Girl of Portici* sent an already restive audience wild and they rushed outside to raise the Brabant flag, traditionally starting the revolution against their Dutch rulers. *Place de la Monnaie.* ☎ *070 23 39 39. www.lamonnaie.be. Tickets 10€–104€. Métro: Bourse. Map p 120.*

Puppet Theater

★★ kids Théâtre Royal de Toone GRAND' PLACE

The puppets and the puppet master are equally famous; the serious plays are performed in a French-based Bruxellois dialect (occasionally in English), and the whole experience in this small theater is not to be missed: Plays from Thursday to Saturday. *21 petite rue des Bouchers.* ☎ *02 513 54 86. www.toone.be. Tickets 10€. Métro: Bourse. Map p 120.* ●

Brussels **Lodging**

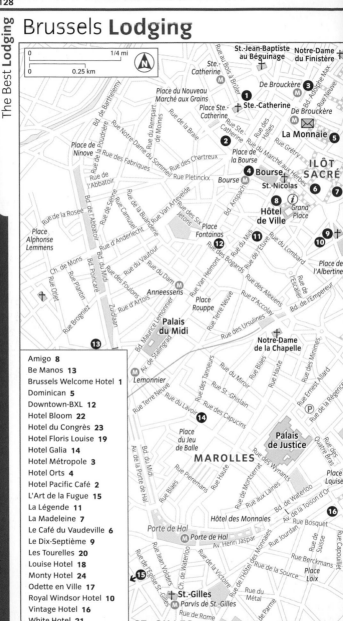

Previous page: Brussels Welcome Hotel.

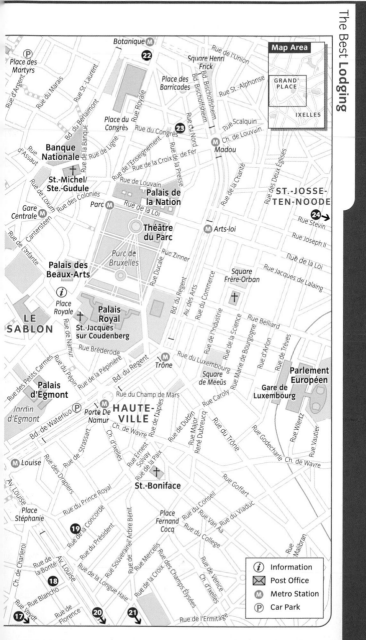

Map Area

GRAND'
PLACE

IXELLES

Botanique **M**
22

Rue de l'Union
Square Henri Frick
Rue St.-Alphonse
Rue de Bischoffsheim
Bd. Bischoffsheim
Rue du Nord
Rue Scalquin
Ch. de Louvain
Place des Barricades
Madou M
Rue de la Charité
ST.-JOSSE-TEN-NOODE
Rue des Deux Églises

P Place des Martyrs
Rue d'Argent
Rue du Marais
Rue St.-Laurent
Rue Royale
Place du Congrès
Rue du Congrès
23
Rue de l'Enseignement
Rue de la Croix de Fer
Rue de la Presse

Banque Nationale
Bd. du Berlaimont
Rue de la Banque
Rue de Ligne
Rue de Louvain
Palais de la Nation

Rue d'Assaut
St.-Michel/ Ste.-Gudule
Rue de Loxum
Rue des Colonies
Parc **M**
Rue de la Loi

Gare Centrale M
Canterstein
Théâtre du Parc
M Arts-loi

Rue de l'Infante
Parc de Bruxelles
Rue Zinner
Palais des Beaux-Arts
Rue Ducale
Rue Stevin
24 →
Rue Joseph II
Rue de la Loi
Rue Jacques de Lalaing

(i)
Place Royale
LE SABLON
Rue de Namur
Palais Royal
St.-Jacques sur Coudenberg
Rue Bréderode
Bd. du Régent
Av. des Arts
Rue du Commerce
Square Frère-Orban
Rue de l'Industrie
Rue de la Science
Rue Belliard
Rue d'Arlon
Rue de Trèves

Rue des Petits Carmes
Rue du Pépin
Rue de la Pépinière
M Trône
Rue du Luxembourg
Rue Marie de Bourgogne
Parlement Européen

Palais d'Egmont
Bd. du Régent
Square de Meeûs
Gare de Luxembourg

Jardin d'Egmont
M Porte De Namur
HAUTE-VILLE
Rue du Champ de Mars
Rue Caroly
Rue Godecharle
Ch. de Wavre

Bd. de Waterloo
Ch. d'Ixelles
Rue de Dublin
Rue Major René Dubreucq
Rue du Trône
Rue Wiertz
Rue Vautier

M Louise
Rue de Stassart
Rue des Drapiers
Rue Ernest Solvay
Rue de la Paix
St.-Boniface
Rue Goffart

Place Stéphanie
Rue de Naples
Rue du Prince Royal
Rue de la Concorde
Rue du Président
Rue Souveraine/Arbre Bénit
Rue Mercelis
Place Fernand Cocq
Rue du Conseil
Rue Van Aa
Rue du Viaduc
Rue du Collège
Rue de Venise
Ch. d'Ixelles

19
Ch. de Charleroi
Rue de la Bonté
Av. Louise
Rue de la Longue Haie
Rue des Champs Élysées

18
Rue Blancho
Rue de Florence
20
21
Rue de l'Ermitage

17
Rue Veydt

(i) Information
✕ Post Office
M Metro Station
P Car Park

Lodging Best Bets

Best **Luxury Hotel**
★★★ Amigo $$$$ *1–3 rue de l'Amigo (p 131)*

Best **Chic Bed & Breakfast**
★★ L'Art de la Fugue $$ *138 rue de Suede (p 133)*

Best for **the Globetrotter**
★★ Brussels Welcome Hotel $$ *23 quai au Bois à Brûler (p 131)*

Best for **Romantics**
★★★ Le Dix-Septième $$$$ *125 rue de la Madeleine (p 133)*

Best **Location for Antique Bargain Hunters**
Hotel Galia $ *15–16 place du Jeu de Balle (p 132)*

Best for **Old-Style Grandeur**
★★★ Hotel Métropole $$$$ *31 place de Brouckère (p 132)*

Best **New Small Boutique Hotel**
★★★ Odette en Ville $$$ *25 rue du Châtelain (p 134)*

Best for **Trendy Shoppers**
★★ Hotel Pacific Café $$ *57 rue Antoine Dansaert (p 132)*

Best **Boutique Hotel**
★★★ Dominican $$$ *9 rue Léopold (p 131)*

Best for **Fashion in the Suburbs**
★★★ Monty Hotel $$$ *101 boulevard Brand-Whitlock (p 133)*

Best **Location for Savvy Eurostar Travelers**
★★ Be Manos $$$ *23–27 square de l'Aviation (p 131)*

Best **Business Hotel**
★★ Hotel Bloom $$ *250 rue Royale (p 132)*

Best **Budget Hotel**
★ Hotel du Congrès $$ *42 rue du Congres (p 132)*

Best for **a Return to Your Schooldays**
★ Les Tourelles $$ *35 avenue Winston-Churchill (p 133)*

Best for **the Fashion Conscious**
★★★ Royal Windsor Hotel $$$$$ *5 rue Duquesnoy (p 134)*

An elegant bedroom in Le Dix-Septième.

Brussels **Lodging A to Z**

Fall in love with the Brussels Welcome Hotel.

★★★ **Amigo** GRAND' PLACE

Brussels' top hotel attracts rap stars and E.U. mandarins alike. The decor expertly mixes classics with modern style, and pictures of Hergé's characters Tintin, Captain Haddock, and Snowy the dog keep you company in every room. The 1958 hotel was built over the remains of a 16th-century prison—Amigo is slang for jail. *1–3 rue de l'Amigo.* ☎ *02 547 47 47. www.hotelamigo.com. 174 units. Doubles 199€–650€. AE, DC, MC, V. Métro: Bourse. Map p 128.*

★★ **Be Manos** GARE DU MIDI

The opening of this smart, trendy boutique hotel near Gare du Midi is indicative of the slow but steady rise of the rather seedy area around the station, set for a huge revamp. Convenience for Eurostar, coupled with a stunning decor, guarantees success for the hotel. *23–27 square de l'Aviation.* ☎ *02 520 65 65. www. bemanos.com. 60 units. Doubles 140€–340€ w/breakfast. AE, DC, MC, V. Métro: Gare du Midi. Map p 128.*

★★ kids **Brussels Welcome Hotel** SAINTE-CATHERINE

I fell in love with this hotel the moment I walked in. Owners Michel and Sophie Smeesters have created a traveler's fantasy. Each room is very stylishly done, decorated with the lanterns, pictures, silks, and tiles the owners have brought back from their own travels; try the vibrant life of Cuba, the cool setting of Zanzibar, or the regal blues and gold of the Egyptian suite. *23 quai au Bois à Brûler.* ☎ *02 219 95 46. www.hotelwelcome.com. 17 units. Doubles 135€–155€ w/ breakfast. AE, DC, MC, V. Métro: Sainte-Catherine. Map p 128.*

★★★ **Dominican** DE BROUCKÈRE

Brussels' latest addition in the super-cool design category recalls its origins—a 15th-century Dominican monastery—in its glorious archways, high ceilings, and courtyard. Stylish rooms are richly colored; calm down in the Turkish bath or Finnish sauna. *9 rue Léopold.* ☎ *02 203 08 07. www.designhotels.com.*

Super-stylish room at the Dominican.

150 units. Doubles 125€–425€. AE, DC, MC, V. Métro: De Brouckère. Map p 128.

★★ Downtown-BXL SAINT-JACQUES   Stylishly decorated in retro chic, with dark colors and striking pictures on the walls, this 19th-century house has just three rooms on three floors. Breakfast is in a delightful room downstairs with an old dresser. Strictly non-smoking. *118 rue du Marché au Charbon.* ☎ *475 29 07 21. www.downtown bxl.com. 3 units. 76€ w/breakfast. MC, V (5€ handling charge). Métro: Anneessens. Map p 128.*

★★ kids Hotel Bloom BOTA-NIQUE   Aimed at the young and fashionable, this refreshing, contemporary hotel has spacious, light, airy rooms with boldly decorated walls painted by young European artists. *250 rue Royale.* ☎ *02 220 66 11. www.hotelbloom.com. 306 units. Doubles 95€–250€ w/breakfast. AE, DC, MC, V. Métro: Botanique. Map p 128.*

★ Hotel du Congrès MADOU   Tucked away in a side street, this hotel has taken over four 19th-century townhouses. Some of the large bedrooms have original

features such as fireplaces. *12 rue du Congrès.* ☎ *02 217 18 90. www. hotelducongres.be. 70 units. Doubles 90€–140€ w/breakfast. AE, DC, MC, V. Métro: Madou. Map p 128.*

Hotel Floris Louise LOUISE   This hotel has comfortable, modern rooms near the smart shops of Avenue Louise. It's quiet with friendly, helpful staff. *59–61 rue Concorde.* ☎ *02 515 00 60. www.florishotels. com. 36 units. Doubles 95€–305€. AE, DC, MC, V. Métro: Louise. Map p 128.*

kids Hotel Galia MAROLLES   Antique hunters couldn't be better placed than here, where the dealers set up their stalls daily. It's a cheerful fairly basic lodging. *15–16 place du Jeu de Balle.* ☎ *02 502 42 43. www.hotelgalia.com. Doubles 75€–85€ w/breakfast. MC, V. Métro: Porte de Hal. Map p 128.*

★★★ Hotel Métropole DE BROUCKÈRE   This opulent hotel opened in 1895 to great excitement, and still has Champagne-bucket loads of late 19th-century style, including original marbled halls, glittering crystal chandeliers, and Gobelin tapestries. Bedrooms are grand; the restaurant is top-notch. *31 place de Brouckère.* ☎ *02 217 23 00. www.metropolehotel.com. 298 units. Doubles 140€–419€ w/breakfast. AE, DC, MC, V. Métro: De Brouckère. Map p 128.*

★★ Hotel Orts ST.-GERY-DANSAERT   This 19th-century building fits perfectly into trendy St.-Géry. Bedrooms are boldly colored and striped, with antique touches such as old lamps and gilt mirrors. *38–40 rue Auguste Orts.* ☎ *02 517 07 18. www.hotelorts.com. 14 units. Doubles 90€–200€. AE, DC, MC, V. Métro: Bourse. Map p 128.*

★★ Hotel Pacific Café ST.-GERY-DANSAERT   The Pacific's simple, but inspired, design features minimal decor and light-colored furnishings. The shower and bathrooms have transparent glass doors that can be hidden from the bedroom by a curtain or door, to add a certain frisson. Breakfast is in the brasserie-style cafe/restaurant. *57 rue Antoine Dansaert.* ☎ *02 213 00 80. www.hotelcafepacific.com. 13 units. Doubles 139€–189€ w/breakfast. AE, MC, V. Métro: Bourse. Map p 128.*

★★ **L'Art de la Fugue** GARE DU MIDI Everything in this very upscale B&B is stylish, from the individually decorated bedrooms to the chic and spacious bathrooms. One room has its own kitchen and most look out over the back garden. There's a communal kitchen. *38 rue de Suède.* ☎ *02 478 69 59 44. www.lartdelafugue.com. 5 units. Doubles 96€–109€ w/breakfast. Métro: Gare du Midi. Map p 128.*

kids La Légende GRAND' PLACE Enter this well-located family-run hotel via a courtyard off a central street. Large bedrooms are decorated with chintz bedspreads and high gloss wooden furniture. *35 rue du Lombard.* ☎ *02 512 82 90. www.hotellalegende.com. 26 units. Doubles 90€–180€ w/breakfast. AE, DC, MC, V. Métro: Bourse. Map p 128.*

La Madeleine GRAND' PLACE Executive rooms at this hotel near the Grand' Place are a decent size and comfortable, though not luxurious. It's a great location, good value for money, and welcoming. *22 rue de la Montagne.* ☎ *02 513 29 73. www.hotel-la-madeleine.be. 52 units. Double 110€ w/breakfast. AE, DC, MC, V. Métro: Gare Centrale. Map p 128.*

★ **Le Café du Vaudeville** GRAND' PLACE Four differently decorated, spacious B&B rooms in the center of the splendid Galeries de la Reine—what could be better for a shopaholic? It's a delightful hideaway. *11–13 galerie de la Reine.* ☎ *02 511 23 45. www.cafeduvaudeville.be. 4 units. Doubles 115€–155€ w/breakfast. AE, MC, V. Métro: Bourse. Map p 128.*

★★★ **Le Dix-Septième** GRAND' PLACE Once the 18th-century residence of the Spanish ambassador, this hotel scores highly for its decor and welcome. Some of the elegant bedrooms have fireplaces and terraces. *25 rue de la Madeleine.* ☎ *02 517 17 17. www.ledixseptieme.be. 24 units. Doubles 150€–270€ w/breakfast. AE, DC, MC, V. Métro: Gare Centrale. Map p 128.*

★ **kids Les Tourelles** UCCLE The 19th-century building with its red brick and black-and-white wooden facade was once a boarding school for genteel young ladies. Now it's a delightful small hotel, decorated in a comfortable, conservative style that wouldn't frighten the pupils. *35 avenue Winston-Churchill.* ☎ *02 344 95 73. www.lestourelles.be. 18 units. Doubles 95€–120€ w/breakfast. AE, MC, V. Trams 3, 90. Map p 128.*

★ **Louise Hotel** ST. GILLES Walking into the foyer takes you back to a former age. Bedrooms are currently being renovated, with plain and simple decor. Good value in an area that's more residential than touristy. *40 rue Veydt.* ☎ *02 537 40 33. www.louisehotel.com. 49 units. Doubles 64€–140€ w/breakfast. AE, DC, MC, V. Métro: Louise. Map p 128.*

★★★ **Monty Hotel** TERVEUREN/MONTGOMERY The Monty burst on to the Brussels scene in 2002 as the first 'design' hotel in the city. Its startling gray and red decor, and contemporary furniture by Ron Arad, Charles Eames, and Philippe Starck, came as a revelation. Other design hotels have opened since, but the Monty keeps its edge.

Monty Hotel was the first 'design hotel' in the city.

101 boulevard Brand-Whitlock.
☎ 02 734 53 36. www.monty-hotel.
be. 18 units. Doubles 99€–195€ w/
breakfast. AE, DC, MC, V. Métro:
Georges-Henri. Map p 128.

★★★ **Odette en Ville** LA CHATE-
LAIN A very chic new boutique
hotel just near Place du Châtelain,
with rooms in black, white, and
grays, and superb bathrooms. The
restaurant is making a name for
itself; and there's a moody bar and
library/lounge decorated by the English owner. 25 rue du Châtelain.
☎ 02 640 26 26. www.chez-odette.
com. 8 units. 250€–425€ w/breakfast.
AE, DC, MC, V. Tram: 81, 92 to Bailli.
Map p 128.

★★★ **Royal Windsor Hotel**
GRAND' PLACE This smart city
hotel has upped the ante for chic by
creating ten 'Fashion Rooms,' each
by a famous Belgian designer. If you
want theatrical, go for the outra-
geous Kaat Tilley room; minimalism

reigns in the Jean-Paul Knott room,
while elegant restraint and great
fashion photographs are displayed
in the Pascale Kervan room. 5 rue
Duquesnoy, ☎ 02 505 55 55. www.
warwickhotels.com. 267 units. Doubles 400€–500€. AE, DC, MC, V.
Métro: Gare Centrale. Map p 128.

★ **kids** **Vintage Hotel** IXELLES
Relive those glorious flared trouser
days at this 1970s-styled hotel. It's
all swirly psychedelic wallpaper and
retro furniture. The wine bar/break-
fast room looks onto a courtyard.
45 rue Dejoncker. ☎ 02 533 99 80.
www.vintagehotel.be. 29 units.
Doubles 95€–155€ w/breakfast. AE,
MC, V. Métro: Louise. Map p 128.

★ **White Hotel** IXELLES Defi-
nitely for those after a design experience, this chic hotel has a white
reception and breakfast room with
white bedrooms shot through with
splashes of color. Lots of design
artifacts in the rooms; funky scoot-
ers are for hire. 212 avenue Louise.
☎ 02 644 29 29. www.thewhite
hotel.be. 53 units. Doubles 90€–
180€ w/breakfast. AE, DC, MV, C.
Tram: 81, 94 to Bailli. Map p 128. ●

Stay in a chic 'fashion room' at the Royal Windsor Hotel.

Waterloo

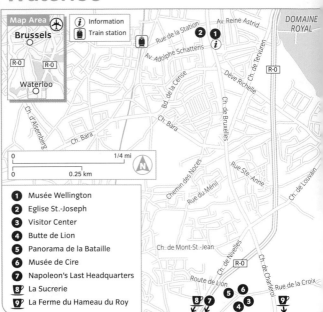

Map Area ✈
Brussels ○

ⓘ Information
🚉 Train station

R-0   R-0

Waterloo ○

Ch. d'Alsemberg

Ch. Bara

Rue de la Station
Av. Adolphe Schattens
Av. Reine Astrid
DOMAINE ROYAL

Ch. de Tervuren
Deve Richelle
R-0

Bd. de la Cense
Ch. de Bruxelles
Ch. Bara

Chemin des Noces
Rue Ste.-Anne
Rue du Ménil

Ch. de Louvain

Ch. de Mont-St.-Jean
R-0
Route de Lion
Ch. de Nivelles
Ch. de Charleroi
Rue de la Croix

0   1/4 mi
0   0.25 km   N

1 Musée Wellington
2 Eglise St.-Joseph
3 Visitor Center
4 Butte de Lion
5 Panorama de la Bataille
6 Musée de Cire
7 Napoleon's Last Headquarters
8 La Sucrerie
9 La Ferme du Hameau du Roy

The Battle of Waterloo, fought on June 18, 1815, was one of the decisive events in European history. Although Napoleon's French forces were better armed, defeat to a British-led alliance that included Dutch, Belgian, and Prussian troops spelled the end of his mighty French Empire. The battlefield sites give a vivid picture of a historic turning point. START: Musée Wellington.

1 ★ kids Musée Wellington.
This museum is dedicated to the English general Arthur Wellesley, Duke of Wellington, also known as the 'Iron Duke,' and is located in the inn where he stayed before the battle. It exhibits a peculiar mix of items: Breastplates riddled with musket holes, plans and models of the battle, busts of his generals, and the canteen trunk of the Chief of Staff of the Dutch army containing personal items such as an elaborate

Previous page: Wellington Museum.

silver egg cup—a reminder that life in the field for the top brass was a replica of comfortable lives at home. Youngsters love the artificial leg of English commander, Lord Uxbridge. The noble lord's leg was amputated after a wound to his knee and buried here. When Uxbridge died in London in 1854, the leg was sent back to be buried with its owner and grateful relatives reciprocated by returning the artificial one. *147 chaussée de Bruxelles.* ☎ *02 357 28 60. www.museewellington.com. Admission 5€ adults, 2€ children*

Musée Wellington.

6–12, also included on the 1815
Pass: see ❸. Apr–Oct daily 9:30am–
6:30pm; Nov–Mar daily 10:30am–
5pm; closed Dec 25, Jan 1.

❷ **Eglise St.-Joseph.** Walk
across the road from the Musée to
the little church of St.-Joseph. It was
built as a royal chapel in the 1680s,
but an extension added after 1815
destroyed all but the original elegant cupola. Inside there's a bust of
Wellington and a monument to the
British soldiers who died at the Battle of Waterloo. Many of the memorial plaques were paid for by
ordinary soldiers in honor of their
officers, the British Army being too
mean—or too poor—to pay for
them. *Chaussée de Bruxelles.* ☎ 02
354 00 11. *Free admission. Daily
8:30am–7pm.*

Take bus W from Chaussée de
Bruxelles to:

❸ **kids Visitor Center.** This center is one of several attractions at
the battlefield's heart, 4km (2.5
miles) south of Waterloo. It gives an
idea of the battle itself and has a

20-minute film explaining the tactics
and action. From here you can climb
the Butte de Lion (❹). *252–254
route du Lion, Braine-l'Alleud.* ☎ 02
385 19 12. www.waterloo1815.be/
en/waterloo. *1815 Pass inc. admission to Musée Wellington, Napoleon's Last Headquarters, Butte de
Lion, Musée de Cire, Panorama, and
2 films: 12€ adults, 6€ children
6–17; plus Battlefield Tour bus (45
min): add 2.60€. Apr–Oct daily
9:30am–6:30pm, Nov–Mar daily
10:30am–5pm; closed Dec 25, Jan 1.*

❹ ★ **Butte de Lion.** The Lion's
Mound is the most striking monument on the battlefield. At 45m (147
ft.) high and constructed in 1823–
26, it commemorates the spot
where Holland's Prince William of
Orange, one of Wellington's Allied
commanders and later King William
II of the Netherlands, was wounded.
315 route du Lion. See ❸.

❺ ★ **Panorama de la Bataille.**
In the age before cinema and televi-
sion, painted panoramas gave the
masses a dramatic impression of
great events. This one was painted

Practical Matters

A regular train service runs from each of Brussels Nord, Centrale, and Midi stations to the suburb of Waterloo, where a signposted 15-minute walk leads you to the Musée Wellington and Eglise St.-Joseph. From across the street in Chaussée de Bruxelles, bus W leaves every 30 minutes to the main battle site at Braine-l'Alleud. The **Maison du Tourisme de Waterloo,** 218 chaussée de Bruxelles (☎ 02 352 09 10; www.waterloo-tourisme.be) is opposite the Musée Wellington. Here you can buy the **1815 Pass** (❸).

in 1912 by French artist Louis Dumoulin and a team of assistants. It's 110m (360 ft.) long and 12m (40 ft.) high and although the quality is hardly Michelangelo, it does give a picture of what French Marshal Ney's attack on the central part of Wellington's army might have looked like. *252–254 route du Lion, Braine-l'Alleud. See* ❸.

❻ **kids** **Musée de Cire.** The Wax Museum is an odd mixture of military items and models of soldiers dressed in the uniforms of 1815. If you're expecting Madame Tussauds, you'll be sorely disappointed. *315–317 route du Lion, Braine-l'Alleud. See* ❸.

❼ **Napoleon's Last Headquarters.** You have to drive or take a taxi to see the French leader's venue on the eve of the battle. On the night of June 17, Napoleon and his immediate staff stayed in this farmhouse, called **Le Caillou.** It's a

small museum with items including his army-issue bed and death mask on display. *66 chaussée de Bruxelles, Vieux-Genappe. ☎ 02 384 24 24. Admission 4€ adults, 2€ children 7–17; also included on 1815 Pass, see* ❸. *Apr–Oct 10am–6:30pm, Nov–Mar 10am–5pm, closed Dec 25, Jan 1.*

❽ There's not much apart from frites and tourist menus around the Butte de Lion. Therefore, I suggest heading back to Waterloo itself to try the vaulted rooms of **La Sucrerie,** 198 chaussée de Tervuren (☎ 02 352 18 18; www.grandhotelwaterloo.warwickhotels.com, $$$) for a tasty meal in glamorous surroundings. Or go into Genappe and the artisanal bakery of ❾ **La Ferme du Hameau du Roy,** 70 chaussée de Bruxelles (☎ 02 387 15 15; www.fermeduhameauduroy.be, $) for simple dishes, pâtisseries, and coffee. ●

The striking 'Butte de Lion' monument.

The Best of **Bruges**

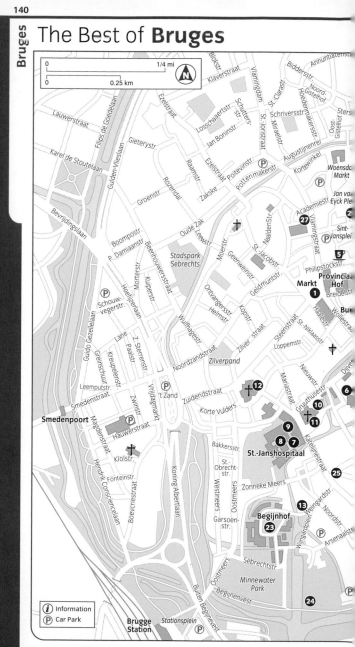

Previous page: Boat tour of the canal, Bruges.

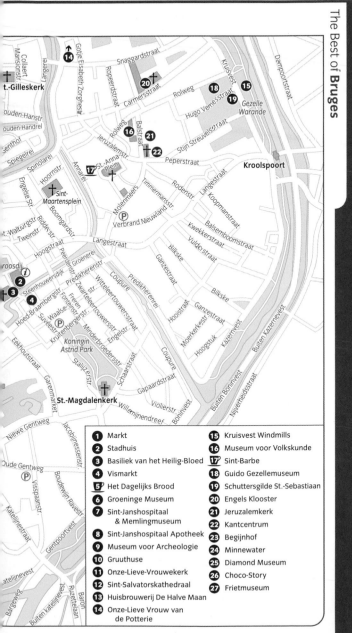

1 Markt	**15** Kruisvest Windmills
2 Stadhuis	**16** Museum voor Volkskunde
3 Basiliek van het Heilig-Bloed	**17** Sint-Barbe
4 Vismarkt	**18** Guido Gezellemuseum
5 Het Dagelijks Brood	**19** Schuttersgilde St.-Sebastiaan
6 Groeninge Museum	**20** Engels Klooster
7 Sint-Janshospitaal & Memlingmuseum	**21** Jeruzalemkerk
8 Sint-Janshospitaal Apotheek	**22** Kantcentrum
9 Museum voor Archeologie	**23** Begijnhof
10 Gruuthuse	**24** Minnewater
11 Onze-Lieve-Vrouwekerk	**25** Diamond Museum
12 Sint-Salvatorskathedraal	**26** Choco-Story
13 Huisbrouwerij De Halve Maan	**27** Frietmuseum
14 Onze-Lieve Vrouw van de Potterie	

Bruges is a stunning city, a place of cobbled streets, magnificent medieval buildings, and quiet canals. In the height of the season it gets overwhelmed by visitors, and so to see the world-class art at your own pace, come in winter. But whenever you visit, try to stay at least one night: Bruges is impossibly romantic when its buildings are illuminated. START: **Markt.**

1 ★★ kids **Markt.** The jousts and public executions that entertained medieval citizens at the heart of their city have given way to horse-drawn carriage rides for tourists, while 17th-century houses have been turned into restaurants and cafes. Their outdoor terraces look onto the center of the marketplace where a statue commemorates local heroes, **Pieter de Coninck** and **Jan Breydel,** who led a bloody revolt against the French in 1302. Dominating the square is the massive 13th-century **Belfort tower,** which rewards anyone with energy to tackle 366 steps with a panoramic rooftop view. 🕐 *45 min. Markt.* ☎ *050 44 87 11. Belfort admission 8€ 26 and over; 6€ 13–25; free for children 12 and under. Daily 9:30am–5pm.*

2 ★★ kids **Stadhuis.** A few steps east of Markt lies Burg, a small square in the center of the city, originally the site of the castle that formed the heart of Bruges. Here you find the 14th-century Stadhuis, which the good burghers used as their government building. They held debates in the Gothic Hall, under its extraordinary carved, vaulted ceiling dating from 1385. The 16th-century **Palace of the Liberty of Bruges** next door is worth a visit for the most impressive baroque chimney in Flanders. Designed in 1528 by Lanceloot Blondeel (1498–1561, it's made from black marble and oak and spans almost one wall of the Renaissance Chamber. 🕐 *45 min. Burg 12.* ☎ *050 44 87 11. Admission to*

Stadhuis in Burg square.

Stadhuis and Palace 2€ 26 and over, free for 25 and under. Stadhuis: daily 9:30am–5pm. Palace: daily 9:30am–12:30pm, 1:30–5pm.

3 ★★ **Basiliek van het Heilig-Bloed.** Inside the Basilica of the Holy Blood, you get a feel for the mystery and power of Catholicism in the form of the most sacred reliquary in Europe—a crystal phial with two drops of Holy blood brought back from the Second Crusade. It's stored in a silver tabernacle and paraded once a year through the streets in a 17th-century gold casket, which is normally on view in the small museum. 🕐 *30 min. Burg 15.* ☎ *050 33 67 92. www.holyblood. org. Museum admission 1.50€ adults and children. Apr–Sept 9:30am–noon, 2–6pm; Oct–Mar 10:30am–noon, 2–4pm. Museum closed Wed pm.*

4 ★ **Vismarkt.** Walk from the Burg through **Blinde Ezelstraat** (Blind Donkey Alley). There was an eponymous inn on the street, but I prefer the alternative story about the street name's origins. The people from Bruges stole Ghent's emblem, a dragon. The dragon's owners arrived with a cart pulled by a donkey but the donkey refused to pass the gate, so the people of Ghent blindfolded the donkey and took the dragon back. The alley leads to the 18th-century fish market—get up early for the fish during the week (only three fishmongers still trade), but at the weekend, there's a small, all-day craft market. ⏲ 20 min. Braamberstraat.

5 kids **Het Dagelijks Brood.** A branch of Le Pain Quotidien chain, this welcoming cafe-cum-shop is an ideal stop for a quick snack or lunch. *Phillipstockstraat 21.* ☎ *050 33 60 50. $.*

6 ★★★ **Groeninge Museum.** Masterpieces depicting the Last Judgment, Virgin with Child, portraits of families and landscapes featuring Bruges are on view in this museum, renowned for its early Flemish and Dutch masters. This world-class museum is quite extensive, so if you want to see a particular painting (my favorite is the *Last Judgment* by Hieronymous Bosch) plan before setting out. Other must-sees include works by Jan van Eyck (1385–1441), Gerard David (1460–1523), and Pieter Brueghel the Younger (1564–1636). Your ticket includes entry into the 18th-century **Arentshuis,** showing works and furniture donated in 1936 by Frank Brangwyn (1867–1956), a relatively unknown British painter born in Bruges. ⏲ *2 hr. Dijver 12.* ☎ *050 44 87 11. www.brugge.be. Admission, inc. Arentshuis, 8€ 26 and over; 1€ 6–25; free for children 5 and under. Tues–Sun 9:30am–5pm. Before big exhibitions, the museum might shut for weeks or months, so check before you travel.*

7 ★★★ **Sint-Janshospitaal & Memlingmuseum.** The lighting is dim inside the red brick-walled, medieval hospital where nuns treated the wounded, the sick, the homeless, and the mad from the 12th century until 1976. In the 15th century, the hospital commissioned paintings from **Hans Memling** (1430–94) and it is these that turn this peaceful place into a cultural gem. I always pick up a free stool so I can sit and contemplate Memling's luminous masterpieces of religious art painted with consummate skill. ⏲ *1 hr. Mariastraat 38.* ☎ *050 44 87 11. Admission 8€ (14€ inc. Onze*

Getting There & Getting Around

From Brussels Gare du Midi, two trains an hour take just under 1 hour to Bruges. By car, Bruges is 10km (6 miles) from Zeebrugge, 15km (9 miles) from Ostend, and 96km (60 miles) from Brussels. The city is small and very compact; you can get everywhere on foot. Many streets are for pedestrians, bicycles, and buses only, so if you come by car, park in one of the parking lots on the outskirts and take a taxi or bus into the center. For more information on buses in Bruges, see p 167.

Sint-Janshospitaal.

Lieve Vrouw ter Potterie, **⑪** *) 26 and over, free for 25 and under. Tues–Sun 9:30am–5pm.*

⑧ ★ **kids Sint-Janshospitaal Apotheek.** When the crowds are overwhelming, this former St. John's Hospital pharmacy is a haven of peace, much as it was in the Middle Ages when it supplied the latest in cutting-edge medicines. Its few rooms are full of chests and shelves of old glass jars and colorful ceramic pots that once contained medieval herbal medicines. ⏱ *15 min. Off Mariastraat, Sint-Janshospitaal. Admission 2€ 26 and over, free for 25 and under. See* **⑦** *.*

⑨ ★ **kids Museum voor Archeologie.** An archeological museum might not seem a place for children, but this one has excellent interactive and audiovisual presentations built around the major finds of Bruges. Upstairs it gets more serious, with pottery shards and Roman glass. ⏱ *30 min. Mariastraat 36A.* ☎ *050 44 87 11. Admission 2€ 26 and over, free for 25 and under. Tues–Sun 9:30am–12:30pm and 1:30–5pm.*

⑩ ★★★ **kids Gruuthuse.** In the 15th century, merchants who grew rich from the privilege of levying a

tax on the *Gruit*, a herbal mix used in brewing, also enjoyed the perk of living in this old mansion. The Lords (known as the 'Lords of the Gruuthuse') lived here in style, with rich tapestries on the walls to keep out the cold, and furniture to impress the neighbors. The now-restored house gives a glimpse of life in a wealthy medieval home. *Dijver 17.* ☎ *050 44 87 11. Admission 6€ 26 and over, free for 25 and under. Tues–Sun 9:30am–5pm.*

⑪ ★★ **Onze-Lieve-Vrouwekerk.** Begun in 1220, this Church of Our Lady took more than 200 years to build. The relative simplicity of the interior makes a good backdrop for its greatest work of art: Michelangelo's *Madonna and Child* is the artist's only sculpture to leave Italy during his lifetime. But there are other treasures: *The Last Supper* (1562) by Pieter Pourbus (1523–84) and the tombs of Charles the Bold, ruler from 1467–77, and his daughter Mary of Burgundy, who tragically died in 1482 aged 25,

Gruuthuse near the Dijver canal.

after falling off her horse. ⏱ *30 min. Mariastraat.* ☎ *050 44 87 11. Museum admission 2€ 26 and over, free for 25 and under. Mon–Sat 9:30am–4:50pm, Sun 1:30–4:50pm.*

⓬ ★★ Sint-Salvatorska-thedraal. Although Bruges' official cathedral, the main attraction here lies in the furnishings and museum rather than the building itself. Look out for the 18th-century tapestries, the extraordinary baroque organ from 1682, and in the museum the *Hippolytus Altarpiece* by Dirk Bouts (1415–75). ⏱ *30 min. Steenstraat.* ☎ *050 33 61 88. www. sintsalvator.be. Free admission to church. Church: Mon 2–6:30pm; Tues–Fri 8:30am–noon, 2–6:30pm; Sat 8:30am–noon, 2–5:30pm; Sun 9am–10:15am, 2–5pm. Treasury admission 2.50€ adults,1.25€ children under 16. Sun–Fri 2–5pm.*

Sint-Salvator's Belfry.

⓭ ★★ Huisbrouwerij De Halve Maan. After all that time spent among the gods, come down to earth with a tour of the only working brewery in Bruges. It's been turning malt and hops into beer since 1856, a process you see during the tour that ends, naturally, with a glass of their particular nectar. ⏱ *45 min. Walplein 26.* ☎ *050 33 26 97. www.halvemaan.be. Admission 5.50€ adults; children 11 and under 2.75€; children 5 and under free. Tours on the hour: Apr–Oct 11am–4pm (Sat to 5pm), Nov–Mar 11am & 3pm (Sat, Sun to 4pm).*

⓮ ★★ Onze-Lieve Vrouw van de Potterie. From the center, the walk along the quiet Potterierei canal takes you northward to this

small, medieval enclave. The hospital here was founded in 1276 to look after the sick and the poor, and to provide shelter for travelers and pilgrims. Its church was associated with the Potters' Guild, and so it was named 'Our Lady of the Pottery.' There's an elegant, slightly over-the-top baroque church, a Lady Chapel with an apparently miraculous statue of the Madonna and Child, the remains of St. Idersbald, abbot of Ter Duinen (d. 1167), a charming cloister, and a little museum. Nothing spectacular, just a tranquil place to hang out. ⏱ *45 min. Potterierei 79.* ☎ *050 44 87 77. Admission 2€ 26 and over, free for 25 and under. Tues–Sun 9:30am–12:30pm & 1:30–5pm.*

⓯ ★ 🅺🅸🅳🆂 Kruisvest Windmills. Once, more than 20 windmills surrounded the city, standing high up on its outer ramparts and forming a skyline familiar from a thousand Old Master paintings. Now just four stand here: **Sint-Janshuismolen,** built in 1770 and used as a flour mill until 1914, and three others brought from other parts of Bruges to stand in line on the grassy slopes. Sint Janshuismolen now operates as both a mill and a museum. ⏱ *30 min. Admission 2€ adults, free for children 12 and under. Apr, Sept Sat, Sun 9:30am–12:30pm, 1:30–5pm. May–Aug Tues–Sun 9:30am–12:30pm & 1:30–5pm.*

⓰ ★★ 🅺🅸🅳🆂 Museum voor Volkskunde. Like most medieval guilds, the Shoemakers looked after their own, building these almshouses in the 17th century to house impoverished shoemakers. Today they make a perfect setting for the Folklore Museum, a series of rooms variously set up as a hatter's, a cobbler's workshop, a tobacconist, and so on. The museum even has its own inn, the 'Black Cat;' perfect for a post-tour beer in a small, secluded garden. *Balstraat 43. ☎ 050 33 00 44. www.brugge.be. Admission 2€ 26 and over, free for 25 and under. Tues–Sun 9:30am–5pm.*

⑰ ★ Sint-Barbe. Just by the Sint-Anna church, this neighborhood stop offers a great daily lunch for 12€, with Belgian dishes made with fresh, seasonal produce. *Sint-Annaplein 29. ☎ 050 33 09 99. www.sintbarbe.be. $.*

⑱ ★ Guido Gezellemuseum. Guido Gezelle (1830–99), one of Flanders' most famous poets, was born in this brick house in 1830. It's very much a literary museum, and so it helps to know something about the poet beforehand, but either way it's a pretty house with a shady romantic garden that helped mold Gezelle's love of nature, a major element in his work. ⏱ *30 min. Rolweg 64. ☎ 050 44 87 66. Admission 2€ 26 and over, free for 25 and under. Tues–Sun 9:30am–12:30pm & 1:30–5pm.*

⑲ ★★ Schuttersgilde St.-Sebastiaan. The Marksmen's Guild of St. Sebastian was particularly powerful—its members were the longbow archers who defended the city of Bruges. They were also Crusaders and incorporated the Cross of Jerusalem in their coat-of-arms. The 16th- and 17th-century guildhouse is now a museum full of paintings, arms, cannons, and gold and silver ornaments. English connections are strong: while the exiled Charles II of England was in Bruges between 1656 and 1658, he was given the title 'King of the Archers'

by the guild. He also founded the company that became the Grenadier Guards here in 1656. ⏱ *30 min. Carmersstraat 174. ☎ 050 33 16 26. www.sebastiaansgilde.be. Free admission. Apr–Sept Tues–Thurs 10am–noon, Sat 2–5pm. Oct–Mar Tues–Thurs, Sat 2–5pm.*

⓴ ★ Engels Klooster. In 1629, English Catholic nuns fled to Bruges and founded their own order here, calling their English convent 'Nazareth' and being financially supported by the English King Charles II's Portuguese wife, Catherine of Braganza. In 1739 the order renovated the church, the only part that visitors can see. It's a strangely English corner of Bruges. ⏱ *30 min. Carmersstraat 85. ☎ 050 33 24 24. Free admission. Daily 2–4pm, 4:30–5:30pm (but variable, phone for details); closed 1st Sun in the month.*

㉑ ★ Jeruzalemkerk. The story of this church originates with a 13th-century chapel funded by the Italian Adornes family who settled in Bruges after serving in the crusade of Guy de Dampierre, Count of Flanders. What you see is the later church built in 1482, based on the Holy Sepulcher in Jerusalem and—unlike other Flemish churches—sporting an

Jeruzalemkerk.

oddly shaped tower. The interior is equally intriguing, with impressive stained-glass windows, the oldest in Bruges dating from 1560, the black marble tomb of the Adornes family (who still own the church), and an altarpiece carved with skulls and demons reminding us all that Hell awaits the ungodly. ⏱ *20 min. Peperstraat.* ☎ *050 33 00 72. Admission, inc. Lace Center, 2.50€ 26 and over, free for 25 and under. Mon–Sat 10am–5pm.*

㉒ ★ **Kantcentrum.** Housed in the Jerusalem almshouses, Bruges' Lace Center keeps alive the Flemish tradition of hand made lace. There are demonstrations every afternoon and you can buy at reasonable prices in the shop. While you're here, visit the nearby artisan lacemakers **'t Apostolientje** (11 Balstraat). *Peperstraat 3A.* ☎ *050 33 00 72. www.kantcentrum.com. Admission, inc. Jeruzalemkerk, 2.50€ 26 and over, free for 25 years and under. Mon–Sat 10am–5pm.*

㉓ ★★ **Begijnhof.** The Begijnhof was founded in 1245 by Margaret Countess of Kanders. Beguines were members of a lay sisterhood who lived like nuns but did not take vows, so they could return to the world when they wished. You may wonder why anyone would want to leave this peaceful, walled complex with its tree-lined canals, garden, and pretty little houses for the uncertainty of life outside. In 1930, the Benedictine sisters took over the Begijnhof but kept the dress of their lay sisters—so you feel as if you have stepped back in time. One house is open as a museum showing the way of life of a Beguine. ⏱ *45 min. Wijngaardplein 1.* ☎ *050 33 00 11. Museum: admission 2€ adults, 1€ children 8–18, free for children under 8. Mon–Sat 10am– 5pm, Sun 2:30–5pm.*

The peaceful houses of Begijnhof.

㉔ ★ 𝗸𝗶𝗱𝘀 **Minnewater.** Today, it's a picturesque park, much beloved by photographers for its background of lake, 15th-century lock gate, house, and 14th century tower, but Minnewater was originally the harbor that connected Bruges' extensive canal network to the sea. The swans that glide so gracefully across the lake have been here since 1448 when the Bruges citizens imprisoned Maximilian of Austria and beheaded his councilor, Pierre Lanchais, whose crest contained the image of a swan. After Maximilian was freed, he ordered the citizens to keep swans on the canals. ⏱ *20 min.*

㉕ ★ 𝗸𝗶𝗱𝘀 **Diamond Museum.** Bruges is Europe's oldest diamond center, though Antwerp and Amsterdam are now better known for the trade. This private museum tells the story of diamonds with models, objects, and a replica workshop of the inventor of diamond polishing in the 15th century (he was from Bruges). Be there at 12:15pm for a demonstration of diamond cutting. ⏱ *45 min. Katelijnestraat 43.*

Minnewater park and lake.

☎ *050 34 20 56. www.diamond museum.be. Admission 7€ (10€ with demonstration) adults, 5€ (8€ with demonstration) children under 17. Daily 10:30am–5:30pm.*

26 ★ **kids** **Choco-Story.** The story of chocolate is located in a house dating from 1480. It's a fascinating and serious overview from its origins to how to make it (plus a taster, of course). Attached is the **Lumina Domestica** telling the story of lamps through the ages; best for those with a lighting passion. ⊕ *45 min. Wijnzakstraat 2.* ☎ *050 61 22 37. www.choco-story.be. Admission 6€ (10€ with the Frietmuseum or Lumina Domestica; 15€ for all three) adults, 4€ (6€ with the Frietmuseum*

or Lumina Domestica; 9€ for all three) children 6–12. Daily 10am–5pm.

27 ★ **kids** **Frietmuseum.** Where else but Belgium, in which the fry is king, would you find a Fries Museum? In fact the museum provides a serious history of the potato as well as the fries they become later in life. It's very well told, with hilarious facts, and little explanations for children. And of course you can end with a cone of perfectly fried *friet. Vlamingstraat 33.* ☎ *050 34 01 050. www. frietmuseum.be. Admission 6€ (10€ with Choco-Story or Lumina Domestica; 15€ for all three) adults, 4€ (6€ with Choco-Story or Lumina Domestica; 9€ for all three) children 6–12. Daily 10am–5pm.*

Bruges Museum & City Passes

Save money by buying multiple entry tickets. An 8€ ticket (1€ for 6- to 25-year-olds) buys you 1-day entry into the following attractions, known collectively as Bruggemuseums: Gruuthuse, Onze-Lieve-Vrouw, Museum voor Archeologie, Stadhuis, Museum voor Volkskunde, Gezellemuseum, the Kruisvest windmills, and Gentpoort. There's also a 3-day ticket at 15€ per adult; free for children 5 and under. Otherwise buy the **Bruges City Card** (www. bruggecitycard.be), which gives you free or discounted admission to all tourist sites in Bruges, plus canal round trips and tours in the City minibus: 48 hours is 33€; 72 hours is 38€.

Where to **Shop**

Accessories

★★★ Delvaux CENTRAL   The world's oldest fine leather luxury goods company has a large corner store looking onto Markt. It's stocked with beautiful (and expensive) bags and leather goods, but a Delvaux bag is an instant entrée into Belgian society. And the firm is still family-owned. *Breidelstraat 2.* ☎ *050 49 01 31. www.delvaux.com. AE, DC, MC, V. Map p 150.*

★★ Kipling CENTRAL   The Belgian company that makes those very useful leather and material bags, with all the pockets you could want, has a good store in central Brussels showcasing the latest designs. *Geldmuntstraat 41.* ☎ *050 34 77 40. www.kipling.com. AE, DC, MC. V. Map p 150.*

Antiquarian Books & Prints

★ G & M Pollentier-Maréchal SOUTH   This dealer of antique prints has a wonderful selection of quality images of Belgium. *Sint-Salvatorskerkhof 8.* ☎ *050 33 18 04. AE, DC, MC. V. Map p 150.*

★ Marc van de Wiele SOUTH   Specializing in illustrated books from the 15th to the 20th century, this is the place for a *Book of Hours* (serious money) and more affordable books. Opening hours are flexible; phone first. *Sint-Salvatorskerkhof 7.* ☎ *050 33 63 17. www.marcvandewiele.com. AE, MC, V. Map p 150.*

Antiques & Interiors

★ Frederick Declerck CENTRAL   This store is a serious and excellent source for 19th-century antique furniture and decorative items. *Hoogstraat 26–28.* ☎ *050 33 83 32. AE, DC, MC, V. Map p 150.*

★ Frederiek Van Pamel CENTRAL   So you want your home to look like a stylish Bruges interior? Check out the furniture and objects here for your new look. *Eiermarkt 3.* ☎ *050 34 42 11. www.frederiekvanpamel.be. AE, MC, V. Map p 150.*

Books

★ De Reyghere CENTRAL   Great, locally revered bookshop with a very wide range of books on all subjects, beautifully displayed in an old-fashioned store. It's also the place for books on Bruges and Belgium. *Markt 12.* ☎ *050 33 34 03. www.dereyghere.be. AE, DC, MC, V. Map p 150.*

Cigars

Jerry's Cigar Bar CENTRAL   Buy cigars and whiskies at the front, and then retire to the bar at the back for imbibing the odd single malt (or a cup of coffee) and smoking a cigar with the locals. *Simon Stevinplein 13.* ☎ *050 33 77 94. www.jerrycigarbar.com. MC, V. Map p 150.*

Comics

★ kids De Striep CENTRAL   Mostly stocks Dutch and French new and secondhand comic books, but there are also some American comics, gadgets, and images. *Katelijnestraat 42.* ☎ *050 33 71 12. www.striepclub.be. DC, MC. V. Map p 150.*

★ kids The Tintin Shop CENTRAL   A smaller version of the store in Brussels (p 46), this shrine to the comic character stocks a range of comic items, including books, clothes, figures, and puzzles. *Steenstraat 3.* ☎ *050 33 42 92. www.tintinshopbrugge.be. AE, DC, MC, V. Map p 150.*

Bruges **Shopping**

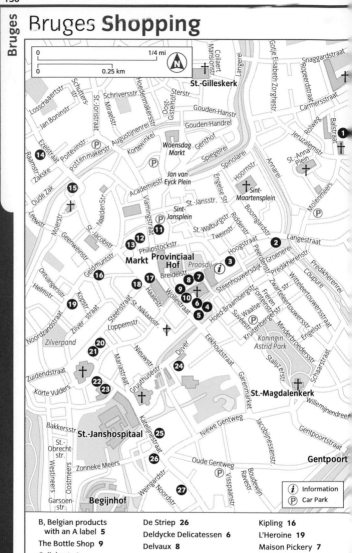

B, Belgian products
with an A label **5**
The Bottle Shop **9**
Callebert **4**
Chocoladehuisje **10**
The Chocolate Line **21**
Chocolatier Dumon **13**
De Krokodil **15**
De Reyghere **17**
De Schacht **27**

De Striep **26**
Deldycke Delicatessen **6**
Delvaux **8**
Frederick Declerck **2**
Frederiek Van Pamel **12**
G & M Pollentier-Maréchal **23**
Jerry's Cigar Bar **20**
Joaquim & Joffre **11**
Kin Gin **14**

Kipling **16**
L'Heroine **19**
Maison Pickery **7**
Marc van de Wiele **22**
Museumshop **24**
Rombaux **3**
Sukerbuyc **25**
't Apostolientje **1**
The Tintin Shop **18**

Design

★★ B, Belgian products with an A label CENTRAL

Founder Katrien van Hulle has sourced top contemporary design from furniture to gadgets, all displayed in a minimal, cool space. *Wollestraat 31.* ☎ *050 49 09 32. www.b-online.be. Mon–Sat 10am–1pm. AE, DC, MC, V. Map p 150.*

★ kids Callebert CENTRAL

You can buy Belgian design and international contemporary furniture here, plus clothes for the ultra-trendy baby. *Wollestraat 25.* ☎ *050 33 50 61. www.callebert.be. AE, DC, MC, V. Map p 150.*

Fashion

Joaquim & Joffre CENTRAL

This Spanish company sells its own fashion brand, Dinou. The clothes are young and fashionable, ideal for the young. *Vlaamingstraat 7.* ☎ *050 33 39 60. AE, DC, MC, V. Map p 150.*

★ L'Heroine CENTRAL

This trendy boutique stocks the top Belgian fashion names. It's a one-stop shop for the likes of Dries Van Noten, Ann Demeulemeester, Rick Owens, and Christian Wijnants. *Noordzandstraat 32.* ☎ *050 33 56 57. AE, DC, MC, V. Map p 150.*

Food & Drink

★ The Bottle Shop CENTRAL

Trappist and Bruges beers: Every name and label you know and a lot you don't. *Wollestraat 13.* ☎ *050 34 99 80. MC, V. Map p 150.*

★★ kids Chocoladehuisje CENTRAL

Come here for inventive handmade chocolates at all prices—at Christmas it's full of chocolate Santas, for Valentine's Day it's hearts all round: Also renowned for truffles and marzipan. *Wollestraat 15.* ☎ *050 34 02 50. www.chocolade*

Chocolate shop window display in Walstraat.

huisjebrugge.be. AE, MC, V. Map p 150.

★★ The Chocolate Line CENTRAL

For some chocolate tastes you wouldn't expect, try this top chocolate shop's 'fusion' line. *Simon Stevinplein 19.* ☎ *050 34 10 90. AE, MC, V. Map p 150.*

★★ Chocolatier Dumon CENTRAL

This artisan chocolate-maker has three stores in Bruges. It's highly rated by locals. *Simon Stevinplein 11, Eiermarkt 6 und Walstraat 6.* ☎ *050 34 62 82. www.chocolatier dumon.be. AE, MC, V. Map p 150.*

★ Deldycke Delicatessen CENTRAL

Uppercrust Belgians buy from this stockist of specialist foods. *Wollestraat 33.* ☎ *050 33 43 35. www.deldycke.be. AE, DC, MC, V. Map p 150.*

★★ Sukerbuyc SOUTH

The chocolate is made on the premises. Ideal gifts at reasonable prices include beautifully decorated boxes made of chocolate. *Katelijnestraat 5.* ☎ *050 33 08 87. www.sukerbuyc. be. No credit cards. Map p 150.*

Gifts

★★ **kids** **Museumshop** CENTRAL Try this store for the wares of several of Bruges' leading museums, from books to fridge magnets, umbrellas to towels. *Arentshof, Dijver 16.* ☎ *050 44 87 36. AE, DC, MC, V. Map p 150.*

Jewelry

★★ **Kin Gin** WEST Textured silver and gold jewelry—some set with precious stones—are made in this atelier/shop owned and run by two young designers: Commission a piece following their knowledgeable and charming advice. *Ezelstraat 27.* ☎ *050 34 19 09. www.kingin.be. AE, MC, V. Map p 150.*

Lace

★★ **Maison Pickery** CENTRAL There are two stores in Paul Lauvers' business, both selling high quality, handmade lace goods and small

Museumshop is great for quirky gifts.

items that make good gifts. The first shop opened in 1871. *Breidelstraat 8 and Wollestraat 30.* ☎ *050 33 07 24. www.maisonpickery.com. AE, MC, V. Map p 150.*

★★ **'t Apostolientje** EAST The 'little apostle' is still a family business, where the husband makes the wooden bobbins and wife and daughters the lace. *Balstraat 11.* ☎ *050 33 78 60. AE, DC, MC, V. Map p 150.*

Music

★★ **Rombaux** CENTRAL Rombaux sells classical CDs, musical instruments, and even busts of your favorite composers. The business is nearly 100 years old and the staff expert. *Mallebergplaats 13.* ☎ *050 33 25 75. www.rombaux.be. MC, V. Map p 150.*

Stationery

★★ **De Schacht** CENTRAL If beautiful Bruges inspires you to draw or paint, come to this welcoming, family-owned store for its wide range of art materials: brushes, paints, pastels, charcoals, and paper as well as stationery. *Katelijnestraat 49.* ☎ *050 33 44 24. www.de-schacht.be. MC, B. Map p 150.*

Toys

★★ **kids** **De Krokodil** CENTRAL Just looking in the windows of this excellent children's toy shop makes me feel better. It's full of well-sourced toys, educational and ecologically sound, but it's not stuffy and the staff are wonderfully open. *Sint-Jakobsstraat 47.* ☎ *050 33 75 79. www.krokodil.be. AE, MC, V. Map p 150.*

Where to **Drink & Dine**

Cafes around the Markt.

★ **Breydel-De Coninc** CENTRAL
SEAFOOD Bright and cheerful sea-food restaurant with lobsters swimming merrily unaware of their fate. *Breidelstraat 24.* ☎ *050 33 97 46. www.breydeldeconinc.be. Entrees 12€–26€. MC, V. Lunch & dinner Thurs–Tues. Map p 154.*

★★ **Cafedraal** WEST *BRASSERIE*
A 15th-century building renovated with verve and style, descriptions that stretch to the cooking. It's an imaginative cut above your average French brasserie menu. *Zilverstraat 38.* ☎ *050 34 08 45. www.cafe draal.be. Entrees 19.50€–34.50€. AE, MC, V. Lunch & dinner Mon–Sat. Map p 154.*

★ **De Botellier** WEST *BELGIAN* A wine shop and split-level restaurant full of odd, delightful artifacts in an old house by the canal. The short menu delivers the likes of duck with orange sauce with gusto, and there's a good wine list. *Sint-Jakobsstraat 63.* ☎ *050 33 18 60. www.debottelier.com. Entrees 13.50€–19.25€, prix fixe 10€–26€. (lunch). MC, V. Lunch Sun–Fri, dinner Tues–Sat. Map p 154.*

★ **De Drie Zintuigen** WEST
BELGIAN Small, welcoming bistro in an old house offering classics such as shrimp croquettes and lamb fillet. *Westmeers 29.* ☎ *050 34 09 94. www.dedriezintuigen.be. Entrees 16€–23€, prix fixe 22€–32€. Lunch & dinner Tues–Sat. AE, MC, V. Map p 154.*

★★★ **De Florentijnen** NORTH
CONTEMPORARY FRENCH The chic interior is a good setting for well-presented, imaginative dishes. *Academiestraat 1.* ☎ *050 67 75 33. www.deflorentijnen.be. Entrees 34€–54€, prix fixe 24€(lunch)–65€. AE, MC, V. Lunch & dinner Tues–Sat; closed mid-July–beginning Aug. Map p 154.*

Bruges **Dining**

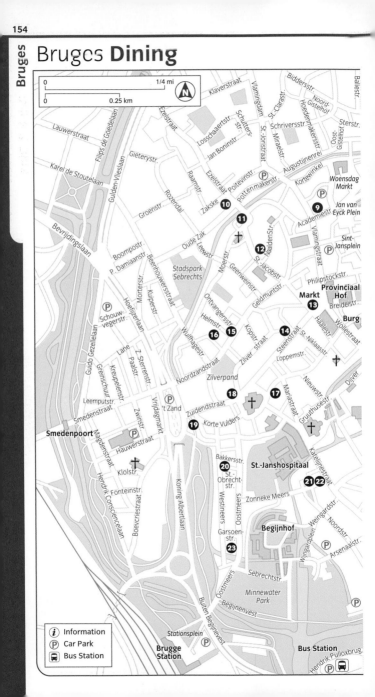

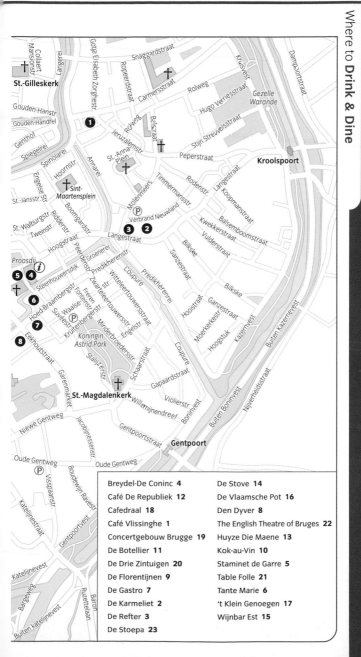

★ **De Gastro** CENTRAL *INTERNA-TIONAL*   Popular restaurant offering a contemporary cuisine of international dishes and tastes, spiced up with Asian touches. *Braambergstraat 6.* ☎ *050 34 15 24. www.degastro.be. Entrees 15.50€–25€, prix fixe 11.50€ (lunch)–41.50€. AE, MC, V. Lunch & dinner Fri–Tues. Map p 154.*

★★★ **De Karmeliet** NORTH *FRENCH/BELGIAN*   Geert Van Hecke was the first Flemish chef to receive three Michelin stars: haute cuisine here is worth every euro. *Langestraat 19.* ☎ *050 33 82 59. www. dekarmeliet.be. Reservations essential. Entrees 60€–110€, prix fixe 80€–180€. AE, DC, MC, V. Lunch & dinner Tues–Sat; closed beginning Oct, end June–beginning July, 1st 2 weeks in Jan. Map p 154.*

★★★ **De Refter** EAST *BRASSE-RIE*   All Brussels cheered when top chef Geert Van Hecke opened this brasserie to serve his superior food at prices for mere mortals: the 35€ menu includes the likes of seafood chowder, Irish stew 'Royal,' and beef tartare. *Molenmeers 2.* ☎ *050 44 49 00. www.bistrorefter.com. Menu 35€. AE, DC, MC, V. Lunch & dinner Tues–Sat; closed beginning Oct, end June–beginning July, 1st 2 weeks in Jan. Map p 154.*

★ **De Stove** CENTRAL *FLEMISH/ SEAFOOD*   Husband-and-wife team Erica and Gino produce good value seafood dishes inside a restored traditional Bruges house. *Kleine Sint-Amandstraat 4.* ☎ *050 33 78 35. www.restaurantdestove.be. Entrees 18€–30€, prix fixe 45€. AE, MC, V. Lunch Sat–Tues, dinner Fri–Tues. Map p 154.*

★ **De Vlaamsche Pot** CENTRAL *FLEMISH*   This cozy restaurant with a family atmosphere offers local specialties such as the famous Flemish stewpot of beef marinated and cooked in beer. *Helmstraat 3–5.*

☎ *050 34 00 86. www.devlaamsche pot.be. Entrees 14€–22€, prix fixe 26€–29€. Wed–Sun noon–midnight. Map p 154.*

★★★ **Den Dyver** CENTRAL *BEL-GIAN*   Family-run restaurant famous for dishes cooked in beer and guaranteed to satisfy the heartiest appetite: Higher-priced menus include wine. *Dijver 5.* ☎ *050 33 60 69. www.dijver.be. Menus 20€ (lunch), 46€–98€. AE, MC, V. Lunch Fri–Tues, dinner Thurs–Tues; closed last week Aug–beginning Sept. Map p 154.*

★ kids **Huyze Die Maene** CEN-TRAL *BRASSERIE*   One of the best of many restaurants lining Markt, it owes its success to well-cooked brasserie dishes and attentive service. *Markt 17.* ☎ *050 33 39 59. www.huyzediemaene.be. Entrees 14€–26€, prix fixe 16€–33€. AE, DC, MC, V. Wed–Mon 9am–11pm. Map p 154.*

★ **Kok-au-Vin** WEST *FRENCH/ BELGIAN*   The casual setting sets the scene for some good Belgian dishes: French-influenced *coq au vin* comes in several guises. *Ezelstraat 19–21.* ☎ *050 33 95 21. www.kok-au-vin.be. Entrees 20€–24€, prix fixe 12€(lunch)–35€. AE, DC, MC, V. Lunch & dinner Fri–Tues. Map p 154.*

★ **Table Folle** CENTRAL *BEL-GIAN*   Decorated in contemporary black, white, and red, you get good classic Belgian dishes here. *Walstraat 11.* ☎ *050 33 00 89. www. tablefolle.be. Entrees 16.50€–22.50€, prix fixe 12.50€–25€ (lunch), 33€. AE, MC, V. Lunch & dinner Thurs–Mon. Closed 2 weeks end Jan–beginning Feb. Map p 154.*

★ **Tante Marie** CENTRAL *TEA ROOM/BRASSERIE*   Good spot opposite the fish market for a satisfying lunch or afternoon tea among the Bruges ladies who lunch. *Vismarkt 7.* ☎ *050 33 03 32.*

www.tantemarie.be. Entrees 10.50€–21€, prix fixe 23.50€ (lunch), 16€ (afternoon tea). AE, MC, V. Daily 10am–10pm (mid-Oct to mid-June to 7pm). Map p 154.

★ **kids** **'t Klein Genoegen** WEST *BISTRO* This little bistro's menu features imaginative salads, pastas, and Belgian classics such as shrimp croquettes. *St. Salvatorkoorstraat 3.* ☎ *050 34 02 38. www.bistrotklein genoegen.be. Entrees 12€–21.50€, prix fixe 30€. AE, MC, V. Lunch & dinner Tues–Sat. Map p 154.*

Pubs, Wine Bars & Lounges
★ **Café De Republiek** CEN-TRAL This buzzing bar is popular with all ages, and has a large terrace and garden, and super-efficient service. *Sint-Jakobsstraat 36.* ☎ *050 34 02 29. www.derepubliek.be. Daily 11am–midnight. Map p 154.*

★ **Café Vlissinghe** CENTRAL It's an old (1515) inn, with the kind of shabby, atmospheric interior that designers strive to make chic: A great venue for your Leffe or other monkish beers. *Blekersstraat 2.*

Café Vlissinghe.

☎ *050 34 37 37. www.cafe vlissinghe.be. Wed–Sat 11am–midnight, Sun 11am–7pm. Map p 154.*

★ **De Stoepa** WEST The atmosphere of an old pub, a great terrace, and good cocktails mean that you fight for space. But persevere; this is a home from home. *Oostmeers 124.* ☎ *050 33 04 54. www. stoepa.be. Tues–Sun 11am–late. Map p 154.*

Staminet de Garre CENTRAL This 16th-century house has just the right wood beams, brick walls, and beer range for a pub of its venerable age. *De Garre 1.* ☎ *050 34 10 29. Daily noon–midnight. Map p 154.*

Wijnbar Est CENTRAL The owner knows her wines, and so be guided by her recommendations: Live jazz and blues every Sunday from 8pm. *Braambergstraat 7.* ☎ *050 33 38 39. www.wijnbarest. be. Thurs–Mon noon–midnight. Map p 154.*

Theater, Music & Dance
Concertgebouw Brugge CEN-TRAL This state-of-the-art concert hall puts on a wide range of music, mainly classical but also jazz, and dance from contemporary to flamenco from international names. Book ahead. *'t Zand 34.* ☎ *070 22 33 02. www.concertgebouw.be. Tickets 5€–30€. Map p 154.*

The English Theatre of Bruges CENTRAL Now in a charming old house next to De Halve Maan brewery, this is the place to see good, professional imported productions from England. An attached bookshop sells English books. *Walplein 23.* ☎ *050 68 79 45. www. tematema.com. Tickets 5€–8€. Map p 154.*

The Best **Lodging**

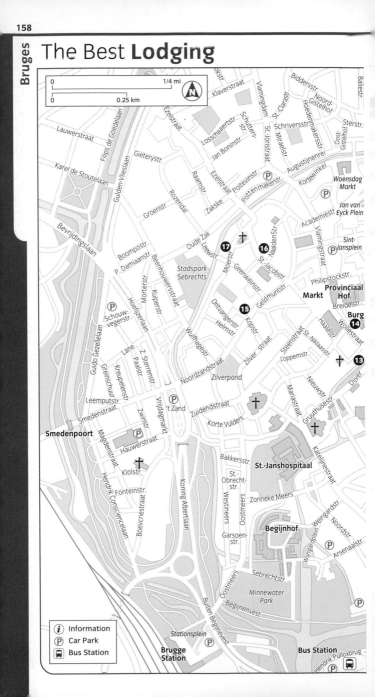

Scale: 0 — 1/4 mi / 0 — 0.25 km

Lauwerstraat
Karel de Stoutelaan
Bevrijdingslaan
Filips de Goedelaan
Gulden-Vlieslaan
Gieterystr.
Groenstr.
Raamstr.
Ezelstraat
Ezelstraat
Rozendal
Zakske
Potevinstr.
Pottenmakerstr.
Klaverstraat
Vlamingdam
Losschaertstr.
Schutters str.
Jan Boninstr.
St.-Joristraat
St.-Clarastr.
Miraelstr.
Schriversstraat
Hoedenmakersstr.
Augustijnenrei
Kortewinkel
Academiestr.
Vlamingstraat
Biddersstr.
Noord-Gistelhof
Oost-Gistelhof
Sterstr.
Baliestr.

Boompostr.
P. Damiaanstr.
Beenhouwersstraat
Morterstr.
Kuiperstr.
Schouw-vegerstr.
Hoeilijerlaan
Guido Gezellelaan
Greinschuur
Lane
Z. Sterrenstr.
Paalstr.
Kreupelenstr.
Leemputstr.
Smedenstraat
Magdenstraat
Hendrik Conscienceleaan
Boevcrnestraat
Fonteinstr.
Klolstr.
Hauwerstraat
Zwinstr.
Vrijdagmarkt
't Zand
Zuidendstraat
Korte Vulders
Noordzandstraat
Zilverpand
Zilver straat
Wulfhagestr.
Ontvangerstr.
Helmstr.
Kopstr.
Geldmuntstr.
Geenwenstr.
St.-Jacobstr.
Naaldenstr.
Moerstr.
Leewstr.
Oude Zak
Stadspark Sebrechts
Woensdag Markt
Jan van Eyck Plein
Sint-Jansplein
Philipstockstr.
Breidelstr.
Markt
Provinciaal Hof
Burg
Wollestraat
Steenstraat
St.-Niklaastr.
L'oppemstr.
Haalestr.
Nieuwstr.
Mariastraat
Gruuthusestr.
Dijver

Smedenpoort

Koning Albertlaan
Bakkersstr.
St.-Obrecht-str.
Westmeers
Oostmeers
Zonneke Meers
St.-Janshospitaal
Garsoen-str.
Begijnenvest
Sebrechtstr.
Begijnhof
Wijngardlein
Wijngardstr.
Noordstr.
Arsenaalstr.
Minnewater Park
Buiten Begijnvest
Oostmeers

Stationsplein
Brugge Station
Bus Station
Hendrik Pulloxbrug

⑰ ⑯ ⑮ ⑭ ⑬

ⓘ	Information
Ⓟ	Car Park
🚍	Bus Station

Where **to Stay**

★ **kids** **Adornes** CENTRAL Four old gabled houses overlooking the canal were turned into a hotel 25 years ago, and are still run by the same family. The rooms in the eaves have beamed ceilings and views; breakfast is served in a delightful room with a fireplace. There's free bike hire and a friendly welcome to returning guests and new arrivals. *Sint-Annarei 26.* ☎ *050 34 13 36. www.adornes.be. 20 units. 120€– 150€. Closed Jan 1–Feb 5. AE, DC, MC, V. Map p 158.*

★ **kids** **Alegria** CENTRAL Owner Véronique de Muynck has lived in Bruges all her life, and is more than happy to help with any requests and information. Her small hotel's six bedrooms are tastefully decorated with individual color schemes; breakfast is served in two high-ceilinged rooms leading onto a pretty enclosed garden. *Sint-Jakobs-straat 34B–C.* ☎ *050 33 09 37. www.alegria-hotel.com. 6 units. Doubles 80€–120€ w/breakfast. MC, V. Map p 158.*

kids **Botaniek** CENTRAL This small hotel in an 18th-century house has nine comfortably furnished rooms. It's a good bet for a moderately priced hotel in the center of Bruges. *Waalsestraat 23.* ☎ *050 34 14 24. www.botaniek.be. 9 units. Doubles 90€–99€ w/breakfast. MC, V. Map p 158.*

Bourgoensch Hof CENTRAL A typical Flemish house down a small alley opposite the Relais Bourgondisch Cruyce looking over the canal—the location is a dream. The decor is simple and functional and there's a small bistro. *Wollestraat 39.* ☎ *050 33 16 45. www.hotelbh. be. 17 units. Doubles 75€–165€ w/ breakfast. AE, MC, V. Map p 158.*

kids **De Loft** CENTRAL A family-run bed and breakfast converted by Thomas Coucke and run by his wife Bieke, who combines bringing up three children with the family business. It's stylish and modern with a simple design, and a real home-from-home welcome and atmosphere. *Timmermansstraat 24.* ☎ *050 33 55 58. www.de-loft.be. 3 units. Doubles 70€–95€ w/breakfast. No credit cards. Map p 158.*

★★ **De Triptiek** CENTRAL This stylish conversion of a 17th-century building that was once three small houses has just three elegantly decorated rooms. There's a living room with a fireplace and a garden for breakfast on a summer's morning. *Nieuwe Gentweg 57.* ☎ *050 61 65 71. 3 units. Doubles 120€–145€ w/ breakfast. No credit cards. Map p 158.*

★★★ **De Tuilerieën** CENTRAL Think four-poster beds, antique furnishings, wooden floors, and luxurious fittings with views onto the Dijver, and as near as you can be to Bruges' museums. It's a favorite with a roll call of the famous running from Denis Roussos to Princess Matilde, via film stars and politicians. *Dijver 7.* ☎ *050 34 36 91. www.hoteltuilerieen.com. 45 units. Doubles 129€–415€. AE, DC, MC, V. Map p 158.*

★★ **Die Swaene** CENTRAL Step straight from the canalside road into a small, pretty lobby in this 18th-century building. Rooms are decorated in flamboyant style; the drawing room is in the old meeting room of the Tailor's Guild, and there's an indoor pool. Book a room in the new wing for waterside views. *Steenhouwersdijk 1.* ☎ *050 34 27 98. www.dieswaene-hotel.com.*

Rooms fit for a duchess in Jan Brito.

30 units. Doubles 195€–295€ w/ breakfast. AE, DC, MC, V. Map p 158.

kids **Jacobs** CENTRAL   Near the market, this good-value hotel in an old building has standard, comfortable rooms decorated in traditional style. *Baliestraat 1.* ☎ *050 33 98 31. www.hoteljacobs.be. 23 units. Doubles 75€–95€ w/breakfast. AE, MC, V. Map p 158.*

★★ **Jan Brito** CENTRAL   The red-brick facade and Dutch gables of this 17th-century house are just what you expect in Bruges, while inside it's been delightfully and unexpectedly restored in Louis XVI style. You can live like a duchess in expensive duplexes in a separate building. Knights' rooms are excellent value at 140€; the Maid's Room at 99€ is a snip. *Freren Fonteinstraat 1.* ☎ *050 33 06 01. www.janbrito.eu. 36 units. Doubles 99€–320€ w/breakfast. AE, DC, MC, V. Map p 158.*

★★★ **Kempinski Hotel Dukes Palace** CENTRAL   Right in the heart of Bruges in a former 15th-century palace, the city's only five-star hotel has a fabulous location and great views. Rooms are elegant and there are conference facilities, a spa and swimming pool, and a delightful bar. *Prinsenhof 9.* ☎ *050 44 78 88. www.kempinski.com/en/*

bruges. 93 units. Doubles 179€– 439€. AE, DC, MC, V. Map p 158.

★★★ **Martin's Orangerie** CENTRAL   Breakfast on the terrace overlooking the canal; rooms full of antiques; a pretty winter garden full of greenery; a bar with more than 20 single malts; and it's all in a former 15th-century convent. What more could you want? *Karthuizerinnenstraat 10.* ☎ *050 34 16 49. www.hotelorangerie. com. 20 units. Doubles 149€–399€. AE, DC, MC, V. Map p 158.*

★★ **Number 11** CENTRAL   A narrow frontage opens into an elegantly decorated house with very stylish rooms. All guests share a generous sitting room with an open fireplace and bookshelves. Breakfast is in the garden in good weather and tea and coffee are available for guests at any time. *Peerdenstraat 11.* ☎ *050 33 06 75. www.number11.be. Doubles 155€– 175€ w/breakfast. MC, V. closed 1st week in Feb. Map p 158.*

★★ **Oud Huis de Peellaert** CENTRAL   This family-owned hotel looks a little like an English country house: it's decorated with comfortable furniture, chandeliers, and striped or floral fabrics. Business clients will appreciate the meeting rooms; holidaymakers might prefer

Bruges

the Wellness Center (free for guests) in a 16th-century vaulted cellar. *Hoogstraat 20.* ☎ *050 33 78 89. www.depeellaert.com. 50 units. Doubles 130€–350€ w/breakfast. AE, DC, MC, V. Map p 158.*

★★★ **The Pand Hotel** CENTRAL Family owned and run as a boutique hotel, the Pand has enormous charm. Its pine-paneled lounges lit by chandeliers welcome sore-footed sightseers; there's a patio garden, sauna, library with an open fire, and a bar with leather armchairs. The refurbished bedrooms are delightful; junior suites have beds with canopies. *Pandreitje 16.* ☎ *050 34 06 66. www.pandhotel.com. 26 units. Doubles 185€–375€. AE, DC, MC, V. Map p 158.*

★★ **Relais Bourgondisch Cruyce** CENTRAL Tucked in an alleyway leading to a spot where two canals meet, this hotel, housed in a romantic, timbered building, featured in the film *In Bruges*. Elegant bedrooms are classically decorated with wooden floors, antiques, and the odd vintage Louis Vuitton trunk. Ask for one of the five superior canalside rooms. *Wollestraat 41–47.* ☎ *050 33 79 26. www.relaisbourgondischcruyce.be. 16 units. Doubles 210€–405€. AE, MC, V. Closed Jan. Map p 158.*

★★ **Walwyck Hotel** CENTRAL Ask for room no. 4 and you get a wonderful corner room looking out over the canal. The hotel is simply but stylishly decorated with a very good breakfast, casual lounge, and helpful staff. It's just outside the center so you see a more residential, local part of the city. *Leeuwstraat 8. Boomgaardstraat 13.* ☎ *050 61 63 60. www.walwyck.com. 18 units. Doubles 80€–120€ w/breakfast. AE, MC, V. Map p 158.* ●

The charming Pand Hotel.

The
Savvy Traveler

Before You Go

Government Tourist Offices

In the U.S.: Belgium-Wallonia: 220 East 42nd St., Room 3402, New York, NY 10017 (☎ 212 758 8130; www.visitbelgium.com). Flanders: New York Times Building, 620 Eighth Ave, 44th floor, New York, NY 10018 (☎ 212 584 2336; www.visit flanders.us). **In Canada:** Belgium-Wallonia: 43 rue de Buade, Bureau 525, Québec City, Québec, CA G1R 4A2 (☎ 418 692 4939; www.visit belgium.com). For Flanders see the New York office. **In the U.K.:** Brussels-Wallonia: 217 Marsh Wall, London E14 9FJ (☎ 020 7537 1132; www.belgiumtheplaceto.be). Tourism Flanders-Brussels: 1A Cavendish Sq, London W1G 0LD (☎ 0207 307 7738. Brochure order line: ☎ 0800 954 5245; www.visitflanders.co.uk).

The Best Times to Go

March to May and **September to late October** are the best times to visit **Brussels,** with fewer tourists than in summer. Brussels is a year-round destination, but in July and August hotel rates are lower because fewer business travelers visit. Note, however, that many restaurants shut for annual holidays at this time. **Bruges** gets very crowded in the summer months, particularly with British visitors. If you prefer a less pressured visit, Bruges is worth considering in winter, with good-value packages on offer and fewer tourists, although remember that some restaurants close for an annual holiday in January. The **festive** season is magical in Bruges, with Christmas markets from early December to the first week in January.

Festivals & Special Events

Also see Festivals & Events, p 124 for the major Brussels arts festivals.

Previous page: The Atomium, Brussels.

SPRING. April sees the **Festival of Fantasy Film, Science Fiction, and Thrillers** (☎ 02 208 03 42, www.bifff.org) for a chance to catch plenty of bad thrillers and odd sci-fi fantasies. For 3 weeks from April to May (dates vary) the **Royal Greenhouses** (p 76, ❺) at Laeken (☎ 02 513 89 40) are open to the public, but be prepared to queue because this is a major event for Bruxellois. Every 2 years (even numbers) the **Zinneke Parade** (☎ 02 214 20 04, www.zinneke.org) pits Brussels' neighborhoods against each other to roll out the best carnival.

In March, Bruges hosts the 11-day **Cinema Novo Film Festival** (www.cinemanovo.be/en) with films from Asia, Africa, and Latin America.

Each May on Ascension Day is the **Heilig-Bloedprocessie** (Procession of the Holy Blood) when Bruges' sacred relic is paraded through the streets (p 142).

SUMMER. July 21 is Belgium's **Independence Day** when you can expect concerts and shows in parks and open-air venues throughout the country. The **Flanders Festival** (www.festival-van-vlaanderen.be) from June to October celebrates classical music in churches, castles, and other venues in around 60 Flemish towns, including Brussels and Bruges. The summer **Couleur Café Festival** (www.couleurcafe. be) in Tour & Taxis (the former center of the European postal service, now an area of restaurants, stores, and exhibitions spaces), is a vibrant, 3-day, live music festival showcasing every genre from world to rap. Summer is celebrated with **Bruxelles Les Bains** (www.bruxelleslesbains.

TEMPERATURE AND RAINFALL IN BELGIUM

	JAN	FEB	MAR	APR	MAY	JUNE
°C	1	4	7	11	13	18
°F	34	40	45	52	56	65
Rainfall (in.)	3	2.5	2	2.5	2.1	2.9
Rainfall (cm)	7.6	6.4	5.1	6.4	5.3	7.4

	JULY	AUG	SEPT	OCT	NOV	DEC
°C	19	18	17	12	7	3
°F	67	65	63	54	45	38
Rainfall (in.)	3.7	3.1	2.4	3.2	2.9	3.4
Rainfall (cm)	9.4	7.9	6.1	8.1	7.4	8.6

be) when an artificial sandy beach draws crowds to the Charleroi Canal for a month from late July. For the **Tapis des Fleurs,** Grand' Place is covered in flowers on a mid-August weekend every 2 years (even numbers).

Bruges rocks to the **Cactus Festival** (www.cactusmusic.be) on the second weekend in July when this 3-day, open-air rock festival disturbs the peace of the Minnewater Park. From late July to August, the **Klinkers Festival** (www.cactusmusic.be) puts on jazz, world music, and films in various open-air Bruges venues.

FALL/AUTUMN. **Europalia** (www.europalia.be) is a remarkable celebration of theater, music, and arts from all around Europe from mid-October to mid-January. **Design September** (www.designseptember.be) is a 3-week long, multi-venue celebration of international design.

You can't get away from the symbol of Brussels on the last weekend in September. The city celebrates the birthday of **Manneken-Pis** when a new suit is presented to him by a foreign dignitary.

WINTER. **Christmas Markets** (early December to early January) are magical, providing a focus for all kinds of local events across

Belgium, but particularly in Bruges. Christmas itself kicks off on **December 6** with the **Fête de Saint Nicolas** (in Wallonia) or the **Feast of Sinterklaas** (Flanders). Christmas is celebrated on **Christmas Eve,** December 24.

January in Brussels sees the city's important international **Antiques Fair** (www.antiques-fair.be) at Tour & Taxis, attracting dealers and buyers from around the world.

The Weather

The climate is generally mild, though October through March can be cold. Spring and Fall/Autumn are generally pleasant, temperate seasons, whereas July and August can become very hot. This being a typical northern European climate, you should come prepared for just about anything.

Useful Websites

- **www.brusselsinternational.be**
  The official site for Brussels International Tourism and Congress, with comprehensive information on mini-trips, packages, culture, and special events.

- **www.belgiumtheplaceto.be**
  Site for French-speaking Brussels and Wallonia for visitors from the U.K. and Ireland.

- **www.visitbelgium.com** Tourism site for U.S. and Canadian visitors.
- **www.visitflanders.be** and **www.visitflanders.us** Website for the Flemish part of Belgium.
- **www.mappy.be** Online maps and journey planner covering Brussels, Bruges, and the rest of Belgium.
- **www.pagesjaunes.be** Online phone directory for businesses and services.
- **www.trabel.com** Information and links to airlines, hotels, and tourist offices.
- **www.artsite.be** Comprehensive site listing the country's main galleries and art museums with links. Also lists private galleries, dealers, and artists.
- **www.beerparadise.be** Official website of the Belgian breweries, with details of brewers, tours, and so on.
- **www.brugge.be** Official Bruges Tourism website, for everything you need to know, do, and book.

Cellphones/Mobiles

The European phone system operates the GSM (Global System for Mobiles) capability. U.K. and Irish mobiles work in Belgium; for U.S. and Canadian visitors to Belgium, check your phone has the GSM standard, and you can then make and receive calls in Belgium. Call your service provider before leaving to ensure that international roaming is switched on, and check charges because they can be high. Remember you're charged for calls you receive on a foreign phone used abroad. **Sim cards** are available from many phone stores as well as at some vending machines in Brussels' stations.

For WAP-enabled phones, download a VoIP application and call from Wi-Fi zones throughout cafes and hotels in both Brussels and Bruges. To reduce charges, switch off data roaming when not needed.

Car Rental

Driving in Brussels and Bruges is not advised. The road system in Brussels is complicated, and much of Bruges is pedestrianized and closed to traffic. If you do need to hire a car, arrange this before you leave. Try **Avis** (www.avis.com), **Budget** (www.budget.com), or **Hertz** (www.hertz.com). **Auto Europe** (www.autoeurope.com) sells a pre-paid voucher to guarantee the rate quoted, locking you in to the current exchange rate.

Getting **There**

By Plane

The major international airport in Brussels is **Zaventem Airport.** For flight information, ☎ 02 753 77 53; www.brusselsairport.be/en. Major airlines fly into Brussels non-stop from London, regional U.K. airports, most major European cities, New York, Philadelphia, Chicago, Atlanta, Washington, Las Vegas, San Francisco, Montreal, and Shanghai. A **taxi** ride from outside the airport terminal to the city center (14km/9 miles) costs around 35€. The cheapest and fastest way into the center is by **train.** Trains run every 15 minutes or so to the three main stations: Bruxelles-Nord, Bruxelles-Centrale, and Bruxelles-Midi. Journey time is 20–30 minutes and it costs 2.60€ each way. An hourly **bus** service, no. 12, runs to Métro

Schuman in the E.U. Quarter and other stops. The journey takes around 30 minutes; tickets cost 1.60€ one way.

Brussels Charleroi Airport, (www.charleroi-airport.com) 60km (37 miles) south of the city, is used by some charter airlines and Ryanair (from London Stansted, and Glasgow Prestwick in the U.K., and Alicante, Bologna, Dublin, Grenoble, Pau, Shannon, and Turin). **Buses** from here to Bruxelles-Midi Station depart regularly, take around 1 hour and cost 10€ one way, 20€ return. They are timed to coincide with Ryanair flights. The Charleroi transfer minibuses (www.charleroitransfer.com) go regularly into central Brussels. 10€ one way.

By Train
Eurostar now runs from London's St. Pancras International. Ten trains a day run to/from London/Brussels. The fastest, non-stop journey takes only 1 hour 57 minutes (stopping at Ashford International and Lille takes a little longer). Tickets start from £69 return if you book well ahead. Buy on their website, www.eurostar.com. Eurostar tickets are valid for free onward travel to Bruges or any other Belgium station. For all European rail travel, including Eurostar, contact **Rail Europe** (U.K. ☎ 0844 848 4064; www.raileurope.co.uk).

By Bus
The cheapest way from London to Brussels is by **Eurolines** (www.eurolines.com) coach. Return fares start at £35; journey time is around 9 hours.

By Car
The main **highways** into Brussels are the E19 and A12 from the north (Amsterdam, Rotterdam, and Antwerp), the E19 south to Paris, and the E40 from Ostend via Ghent.

To Bruges
See The Best of Bruges, Practical Matters, p 64.

Getting **Around**

By Public Transport
Public transport in Brussels is run by the **STIB** (Société des Transports Intercommunaux Bruxellois), ☎ 02 515 20 00, www.stib.be. Maps showing all forms of transport are available free from many Métro stations and the Tourist Office (see p 164). The revamped **Métro** has six lines and is fast and convenient. The **Pré-métro** is part of the tram network and runs underground from Bruxelles-Nord through De Brouckère and Bourse to Bruxelles-Midi, Porte de Hal, and farther south.

Trams are a good way to travel around. You can only board at tram stops; to get off, press the bell. Local **trains** run by **Belgian** **Railways** (SNCB, www.b-rail.be) connect the inner city with the suburbs, though these are rarely used by visitors. **Buses** run throughout the center, and offer a limited night service. **De Lijn** (www.delijn.be) operates from the center to Flemish-speaking communities around the capital, including Bruges. **TEC** (www.tec-wl.be) serves the French-speaking areas to the south.

Tickets can be used on tram, bus, and Métro, which are all part of STIB. Buy before you board. Children aged 6 and over pay full fare. Tickets cost 1.70€ for one journey, 2€ on-board. It is better to buy multiple tickets: five journeys cost 7.30€, 10 journeys 12.30€. A 1-day card for unlimited travel is 4.50€; a 3-day card is 9€.

The **Brussels Card** (www.brusselscard.be) gives you travel and reduced admission to the city's museums and bus tours, and discounts at restaurants and stores. It's available for 24 (24€), 48 (34€), or 72 hours (40€).

In **Bruges,** main bus stops are at the railway station, Markt, Wollestraat, and Kuipersstraat. Buses from the train station to the center are nos. 1, 3, 4, 6, 11, 13, 14, 16. Bruges has no subway or trams. Most city buses depart from the bus station beside the rail station, or from a secondary station at 't Zand, and many buses stop in the center at the Markt. Schedules are prominently posted. A **Daypass** giving unlimited travel on all city buses is 2.90€ and can be bought on the bus, or at the booths at the bus stations; you only have to take three buses to make it worthwhile over purchasing single-journey tickets at 1€ each. For information on the city and regional bus service operated by the **De Lijn** company: ☎ 070 22 02 00; www.delijn.be.

By Taxi

Taxis can be picked up at taxi stands. There is an initial fixed fee of 2.40€ (day), 4.40€ (night), and then 1.35€ per kilometer (double at night). If you need to phone for a cab, try **Taxis Vert** (☎ 02 349 49 49; taxisvertsbe) or **Taxis Bleus** (☎ 02 268 00 00; www.taxisbleus.be).

In **Bruges** you can take a taxi from the train station or the Markt ranks, or call **Bruges Taxi Services** (☎ 050 33 44 55 in English). There is a fixed fee of 2.40€, and then 1.25€ per kilometer; at night an extra 2€ is added.

On Foot

Brussels is a good city to walk around, though surprisingly hilly.

Bruges is made for walking: much of its compact center is pedestrianized.

By Bicycle

Brussels now has an extensive bicycle network and a city-wide renting scheme. Rent short-term, low-cost bikes at any of the 180 **'Villo'** (http://en.villo.be/) rental locations in the streets. You need a Smart card (electronic chip and pin number). Registration is 1.50€ for a day, 7€ for a week. First half hour is free, and then .50€ per half hour. Or take a tour with a guide from **Pro Vélo** (☎ 02 502 73 55; www.provelo.org) who also rent cycles.

Bruges is ideal for renting a bicycle. You can hire one from the railway station, Station Square (☎ 050 30 23 29); plus **De Ketting,** 23 Gentpoorstraat (☎ 050 34 41 96); or **Eric Popelier,** 26 Mariastraat (☎ 050 34 32 62). You need to leave a deposit (around 20€) and produce a photo ID card or passport. Rates vary from around 5€–6€ per hour to daily rates of around 10€. Many hotels also rent bicycles or provide one free for your stay. Touring by bicycle on a guided tour is a good way to see the city and surrounding countryside. Contact **Pink Bear** (English) on ☎ 050 61 66 86, www.pinkbear.freeservers.com; or **QuasiMundo,** (☎ 050 33 07 75; www.quasimundo.com).

Fast **Facts**

ACCOMMODATION **Brussels** is geared to the business traveler, which is good news for leisure visitors. Hotels offer competitive rates in July and August and at weekends all year; the cost of staying at a top hotel can fall by 60%. Useful advance booking services include **Resotel** (☎ 02 779 39 39; www.resotel.be). The Tourist Office has a free, same-day reservation service (see Tourist Information, p 164). For bed and breakfast, try **Bed & Brussels** (☎ 02 646 07 37; www.bnb-brussels. be); for luxury hotels, **Leading Hotels of the World** (☎ U.S. & Canada: 1-800-745-8883; U.K. & Europe: ☎ 00800 1010 1111; www. lhw.com).

Bruges gets booked up in summer but also has many good bed and breakfasts. The **Bruges Tourist Office** offers excellent value winter packages. They also operate a hotel booking service via their website, www.brugge.be. Also see www. hotels-brugge.org. For a luxury hotel choice, try **Small Luxury Hotels of the World** (www.slh. com).

ATMS Maestro, Cirrus, and Visa cards are accepted at all ATMs. Exchange bureaux open later than banks but charge higher commission rates. Exchange bureaux are at **CBC**, 7 Grand' Place (24 hr) and the three major railway stations.

BANKS Most banks are open Mon–Fri 9am–4pm (some to 5pm).

BIKE RENTALS See 'By Bicycle,' above.

BUSINESS HOURS Stores are mostly open Monday to Saturday 10am to 6pm. On Sundays patisseries and specialist food shops are open in the mornings, and all tourist stores around the main sights open every day. Most public museums and galleries are closed on Mondays.

CITY PASSES For details on the Brussels Card, see p 168, and for the Bruges Card, see p 168.

CLIMATE See 'The Weather,' p 165.

CONSULATES & EMBASSIES **U.S. Embassy,** 27 bd du Régent, ☎ 02 508 21 11, www.belgium. usembassy.gov. **Canadian Embassy,** 2 avenue de Tervuren, ☎ 02 741 06 11, dfait-maeci-gc.ca/brussels. **U.K. Embassy,** 85 rue d'Arlon, ☎ 02 287 62 11, www.britishembassy.gov.uk/ brussels. **Irish Embassy,** 50 rue Wiertz, ☎ 02 235 66 76. **Australian Embassy,** 6–8 rue Guimard, ☎ 02 286 05 00. **New Zealand Embassy,** 1 square de Meeus, ☎ 02 512 10 40, www.nzembassy.com.

CUSTOMS E.U. nationals can bring in and out unlimited tax-paid goods, as long as these are considered to be for your 'own use.' Non-E.U. nationals can bring in, duty free, 200 cigarettes, 50 cigars, 2 liters of wine, and 1 liter of alcohol. Customs officials are lenient about general merchandise.

ELECTRICITY The current is 220 AC, 50Hz, with standard European-style two-pin plugs. Adaptors can be bought locally, but it is easier and cheaper to buy a multi-purpose traveling adaptor before you leave. U.S. visitors also need a voltage converter.

EMBASSIES See 'Consulates & Embassies.'

EMERGENCIES For ambulances, medical emergencies or fire services, ☎ 100. For **police,** ☎ 101. For an **emergency doctor,** ☎ 100 or ☎ 02 479 18 18 (Brussels only). For dental emergencies out of hours, ☎ 02 426 10 26. Pan European SOS ☎ 112.

FAMILY TRAVEL The major national websites give good advice (see Useful Websites p 165).

GAY & LESBIAN TRAVELERS There are many gay associations in

Brussels. For information, see www.telsquols.be. **The Rainbow House,** 42 rue Marché au Charbon (☎ 02 503 59 90; www.rainbowhouse.be) is a meeting point for gays and lesbians.

HOLIDAYS Public holidays: January 1 (New Year's Day), March/April (Easter Monday), May 1 (Labor Day), May Ascension Day, Whit Monday, July 21 (Independence Day), August 15 (Assumption), November 1 (All Saints), November 11 (Armistice Day), December 25 (Christmas Day).

HOSPITALS If you need a hospital in an emergency, ☎ 100.

INTERNET/WI-FI There are plenty of Internet cafes in both cities, and most hotels now have wireless access. An increasing number offer wireless for free.

LOST PROPERTY If your credit cards are stolen, call your card company immediately and file a report with the police. For lost cards: **AmEx,** ☎ (+44) 01273 696 933 (U.K.) or (+1) 800 268 9824 (U.S.); **Diners Club,** ☎ 02 626 50 04, 0800 244 0244; **Eurocard/MasterCard,** ☎ 0800 1 5096; **Visa,** ☎ 0800 1 8397. For property lost on the **Métro,** ☎ 02 515 23 94; for property lost on **trains,** ☎ 02 224 61 12; general lost and found office ☎ 02 274 16 90. To report a crime, ☎ 02 279 79 79.

MAIL & POSTAGE Post offices are usually open Monday to Friday, 9am to 5pm. Post offices with late hours include **Bruxelles-Midi,** 48a avenue Fonsny, ☎ 02 524 43 08 (Mon–Fri 7am–10pm; Sat 10am–7pm; Sun 11am–7pm); **Centre Monnaie,** place de la Monnaie, ☎ 02 226 2111 (Mon–Fri 8:30am–7pm; Sat 9am–3pm). Tobacconists also sell stamps.

MONEY The currency of Belgium is the euro, which can be used in most other E.U. countries. Denominations of notes are 5€, 10€, 20€, 50€, 100€, 200€, and 500€. The euro comprises 100 cents. There are coins of 1, 2, 5, 10, 20, and 50 cents, and 1€ and 2€ coins.

NEWSPAPERS & MAGAZINES English-language newspapers are available at most kiosks and stores. One of the best guides to events is the weekly English-language **Bulletin Unlimited** and monthly **Bulletin.**

PASSPORTS If your passport is stolen, contact your local Embassy immediately (see Consulates & Embassies).

PHARMACIES A list of 24-hour pharmacies and doctors is posted on every pharmacy.

SAFETY Violent crime is rare in Brussels and Bruges, but there is a lot of minor, opportunistic crime. Be careful of your bag at all times and wary of pickpockets in crowds near the major sights.

SENIOR TRAVELERS Visitors over the age of 60 qualify for reduced admission to theaters, museums, and attractions. Take your passport or some other proof of age.

SMOKING Smoking is now only allowed in restaurants in a separate room. Smoking is still allowed in bars and clubs, though they must provide a non-smoking zone. Smoking is not allowed in confined public spaces such as railway stations and on public transport.

TAXES Belgian value-added (VAT) tax is 21%. Non-E.U. citizens can claim it back if they spend over a certain amount in a store that participates in the VAT refund program. For more information see www.globalrefund.com.

TELEPHONES For national telephone enquiries, call ☎ 1307. International telephone enquiries: ☎ 1304; International operator assistance, ☎ 1324. The local code for Brussels is 02; for Bruges it's 050. Telephone codes from Brussels (area code minus zero + number): to Australia ☎ 0061; to the U.K. ☎ 0044; to the U.S. and Canada ☎ 001. Telephoning from abroad: from the U.K. and Ireland ☎ 00 + 32 + 2 (Brussels) and ☎ 00 + 32 + 50 (Bruges) + number; From the U.S. and Canada ☎ 011 + 32 + 2 (Brussels) and ☎ 011 + 32 + 50 (Bruges) + number.

See also Cellphones/Mobiles, p 166.

TIME Belgium is in the Central European Time Zone, 1 hour ahead of Greenwich Mean Time.

TIPPING Restaurants and bars usually include a tip in the price of food and drinks. If you have particularly good service, add 5%. You should leave some small change on your table in cafes and bars. In taxis, round up the total by 10–15%, but note that metered taxis include the tip in the fare.

TOILETS Public toilets are kept clean by attendants who expect a tip: 1€ is customary.

TOURIST INFORMATION In **Brussels: Brussels International Tourism & Congress (BITC),** 2–4 rue Royale, ☎ 025 13 89 40, and Hôtel de Ville, Grand' Place, ☎ 02 513 89 40, www.brusselsinternational.be.

In **Bruges: In & Uit Brugge,** Concertgebouw, 34 't Zand, ☎ 050 44 46 46. There is a small tourist information booth in Bruges railway station, off the main entrance lobby.

TRAVELERS WITH DISABILITIES Brussels is not an easy city for the disabled; its cobbled streets, narrow pavements, and hills are a challenge. Trains and trams are not well equipped. The **Accessible Info** point is useful for information: 61 rue du Marché aux Herbes, ☎ 070 23 30 50, www.accessinfo.be. Before you go, check out www.able-travel.com/world_guide/belgium.php for help with accessibility.

A Brief **History**

A.D. **15** The Roman province Galia Belgica is established.

500–721 The Frankish Merovingian dynasty rules the area.

580 Saint Géry, Bishop of Cambrai builds a chapel in present-day Saint Géry in Brussels, which now marks the center of the city.

751–987 The Carolingian dynasty of the Franks rule.

843 After wars between the heirs of Charlemagne, the Treaty of Verdun splits the Holy Roman Empire along the River Scheldt, creating what will become the two separate areas of Flanders and Wallonia.

979 The official founding of Brussels by Charles, Duke of Lorraine.

1128 Bruges is given a city charter. Access to the North Sea helps start Bruges' Golden Age, with the city vastly enriched through wool and cloth trade with England.

1300 The French king Philip the Fair seizes Flanders, despite the 1302 Battle of the Golden Spurs when the French were beaten, largely due to two Bruges heroes, Pieter de Coninck and Jan Breydel.

1337–1453 The Hundred Years War between the French and the English involves Flemish cities such as Bruges who side with their trading partners, the English.

14TH CENTURY Brussels grows wealthy as a trade center. In 1379 the defensive city walls are completed. The city becomes the focus of what's known as the Low Countries.

1384–1515 Through marriage, the Dukes of Burgundy take over Flanders and then most of the Low Countries.

1419–67 The reign of Philip the Good is a golden age for Brussels and Bruges. The arts flourish.

1477 The Spanish Habsburgs gain control through marriage. During Charles V's rule, Brussels becomes the center of his Empire.

1500 The Zwin channel to the North Sea, which gave Bruges its prosperity, starts to silt up and Antwerp takes over. Until the late 19th century, Bruges is forgotten, its buildings left in a time warp.

1556–98 Philip II's rule from Spain proves disastrous. During his reign, the Reformation leads to bitter fighting between Protestants and Spanish Catholics.

1695 French King Louis XIV attacks Brussels, destroying Grand' Place and surrounds.

1741–90 The reign of Charles of Lorraine is another period of stability and prosperity for Brussels.

1790 The French Revolution of 1789 encourages the Flemish to revolt against their Austrian rulers.

1794 The French Revolutionary Army defeats the Austrians and in 1795 Belgium falls to French rule.

1815 Napoleon is finally defeated at Waterloo. The Congress of Vienna gives Belgium to the Netherlands and William Prince of Orange is declared King William I.

1830 A performance of a patriotic opera in Brussels' Théâtre de la Monnaie incites a successful rebellion against Dutch rule.

1831 The international community accepts Belgian independence at the London Conference. Léopold of Saxe-Coburg becomes King Léopold I (1831–65).

1865–1909 King Léopold II's reign is known for rapid industrialization and the enriching of Belgium through the Industrial Revolution, the country's massive coal reserves, and the Belgian Congo (acquired in the 1880s).

LATE 19TH CENTURY Interest in Bruges, the 'Sleeping City,' is rekindled by visitors such as William Wordsworth and Henry Wadsworth Longfellow, who discover a city untouched since the Middle Ages. Major construction projects linking Zeebrugge and Bruges give the city a new lease of economic life.

1909–34 King Albert I rules.

1914–18 World War I: Germany overruns much of the country. Ypres becomes a byword for the senselessness of war.

1934–51 Rule of King Léopold III.

1940–45 World War II: Belgium is again occupied by Germany.

1951 Léopold III, suspected of collaboration, is forced to abdicate in favor of his son King Baudoin I (ruled 1951–93).

1950S Economic boom for Bruges and Brussels.	**2002** Bruges is declared 'European Capital of Culture' for 2002.
1957 The Treaty of Rome sets up the European Economic Community; Brussels is made the headquarters.	**2007** Brussels celebrates 50 years of the Treaty of Rome.
1977 The federal regions of Brussels, Flanders, and Wallonia are established, emphasizing the difference between the Flemish (Dutch) and Walloons (French).	**2009** Prime Minister Herman von Rompuy takes over as President of the European Council.
1989 The Brussels conurbation becomes the autonomous Bruxelles-Capitale Region.	**2010** The movement to split Belgium into two countries, one Flemish, the other French, results in the government resigning four times, leaving the country effectively leaderless during those periods.
1993 Albert II becomes King of the Belgians on the death of Baudoin I.	**2010** In July, Belgium takes over the 6-month European Union presidency.

Art & Architecture Highlights

The Middle Ages (1200s–1500s)

The Romanesque period (11th–12th centuries) was marked by the development of ecclesiastical architecture, mainly influenced by France, though with characteristic elements such as the solid tower seen at Notre-Dame de la Chapelle. But it was the Gothic style of the 13th–15th centuries that produced truly remarkable buildings in the Low Countries. Civic pride took over from religious fervor, and the massive belfries towering over impressive market places (particularly in Brussels and Bruges), the covered markets, guildhalls, and fine town halls (the Stadhuis in Bruges is the leading example), showed off the economic and artistic wealth of Flanders. Because Bruges became an ignored backwater for centuries after trade routes moved elsewhere, buildings such as the Stadhuis have been left just as they were built in the Middle Ages.

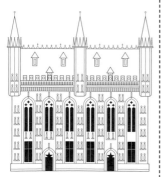

Stadhuis, Bruges.

The Flemish Primitives

At the same time, Flemish painting enjoyed its golden age with artists such as Jan van Eyck (1339–1441), Rogier van der Weyden (1399–1464), who was appointed official painter to Brussels in 1436, Dirk Bouts (1415–75), and Hans Memling (ca.1430–94). They are gathered together in the Musée Royaux des Beaux Arts in Brussels, and in Bruges at the Groeninge Museum and Sint-Janshospitaal.

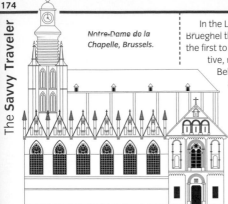

Notre-Dame de la
Chapelle, Brussels.

In the Low Countries, Pieter Brueghel the Elder (ca. 1525–69) was the first to paint in oil using perspective, realistic details, and light. Belonging to the same generation were the Bruges artist Pieter Pourbus (ca. 1523–84), Quentin Metsys (1466–1530), and Jan Gossaert (1478–1532). Pieter Brueghel the Younger (1564–1638) copied much of his father's work; his younger brother, Jan 'Velvet' Brueghel (1568–1625), is known for landscapes and delicate flower paintings.

The Renaissance

Bridging the medieval and the modern worlds, the Renaissance was led by Italy. The Low Countries were largely untouched, continuing their own particular architectural style, with Renaissance motifs added to buildings that remained characterized by traditional forms such as step gables. In painting, too, many artists remained relatively untouched by the style of Italian High Renaissance masters such as Titian.

The 17th & 18th Centuries

Pieter Paul Rubens (1577–1640) dominated baroque painting in Europe; the artistic center of the Low Countries moved from Bruges to Antwerp, where he lived and worked. Other painters of note were Anthony van Dyck (1599–1641) who lived in England from 1632 and Jacob Jordaens (1538–1678). In architecture, the flowing baroque style can be seen in churches such as St.-Jean-Baptiste au Béguinage; in civic architecture, the style was enthusiastically adopted, producing masterpieces such as the Grand' Place in Brussels with its exuberant buildings and flamboyant decorative features.

The 19th & 20th Centuries

The baroque style continued in ecclesiastical buildings, but by the end of the 18th century neoclassicism began to spread, most notably with the Place Royale in Brussels. Neoclassicism in art was represented by François-Joseph Navez (1787–1869), a pupil of French painter Jacques-Louis David (1748–1825), who spent his last years in Brussels. Belgian independence in 1830 gave a new impetus, and the past was evoked in a wave of Romanticism,

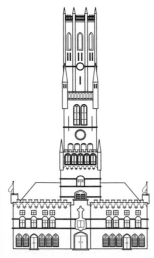

Belfort, Bruges.

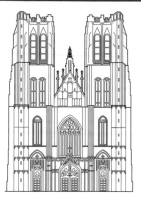

Cathédrale St.-Michel/Ste.-Gudule, Brussels.

which emphasized emotional intensity and passion. Belgian art later found expression in Realism with Constantin Meunier (1831–1905), who painted the misery and heroism of the Industrial Revolution. Major new movements such as Impressionism were largely ignored, but Symbolism took hold in Belgium, epitomized by the strange paintings of Fernand Khnopff (1858–1921).

Fauvism as an artistic form, a development from Impressionism characterized by strong colors, is associated here with Rik Wouters (1882–1916). His

contemporary Constant Permeke (1886–1952) is known for vigorous landscapes and emotional figures. But René Magritte (1898–1967) remains Belgium's most influential and best-known artist of the period for his fantastical, precisely defined painted worlds. His contribution to 20th-century art is acknowledged with the new René Magritte Museum in the Musée Royaux des Beaux-Arts (p 63).

Art Nouveau

Art Nouveau architecture reached its height in Brussels. Victor Horta (1861–1947) first developed the style with his 1893 design for the Hôtel Tassel. Brussels remains one of Europe's great Art Nouveau cities, with many private houses and public buildings exhibiting this undulating, curving, seductive style. See p 32.

Hôtel de Ville, Grand' Place, Brussels.

Useful Phrases & Menu Terms

Belgium has two main languages, reflecting the rough divide between the north and the south. French is spoken in the south, and Flemish, a kind of Dutch called *Vlaams* in Belgium, is the language of the north. In Brussels the predominant language is French, although many people are bilingual; in Bruges, it's Flemish. However, you'll find most people in both Brussels and Bruges speak very good English.

Everyday Phrases

ENGLISH	FRENCH	FLEMISH
Good day	Bonjour	Goedendag
How are you?	Comment allez-vous?	Hoe maakt u het?
Goodbye	Au revoir	Tot ziens
Thank you	Merci	Dank u
Please	S'il vous plait	Alstublieft
I don't know	Je ne sais pas	Ik weet het niet
Yes/No	Oui/non	Ja/nee
How much?	Combien?	Hoeveel?
I don't understand	Je ne comprends pas	Ik begrijp het niet
I can't speak French	Je ne parle pas Français	Ik spreek geen Frans
Watch out!	Attention!	Pas op!
Where is the toilet?	Ou sont les toilettes?	Waar is het toilet?
Ladies	Dames	Damestoilet
Gents	Messieurs	Herentoilet

Numbers

ENGLISH	FRENCH	FLEMISH
1	Un	Een
2	Deux	Twee
3	Trois	Drie
4	Quatre	Vier
5	Cinq	Vijf
6	Six	Zes
7	Sept	Zeven
8	Huit	Acht
9	Neuf	Negen
10	Dix	Tien
11	Onze	Elf
12	Douze	Twaalf
13	Treize	Dertien
14	Quatorze	Veertien
15	Quinze	Vijftien
16	Seize	Zestien
17	Dix-sept	Zeventien
18	Dix-huit	Achttien
19	Dix-neuf	Negentien
20	Vingt	Twintig

Days of the Week

ENGLISH	FRENCH	FLEMISH
Monday	Lundi	Maandag
Tuesday	Mardi	Dinsdag
Wednesday	Mercredi	Woensdag
Thursday	Jeudi	Donderdag
Friday	Vendredi	Vrijdag
Saturday	Samedi	Zaterdag
Sunday	Dimanche	Zondag

Food & Drink

ENGLISH	FRENCH	FLEMISH
Breakfast	Petit déjeuner	Ontbijt
Lunch	Déjeuner	Middagmaal
Dinner	Diner	Avondeten
A bottle of wine	Une bouteille de vin	Een fles wijn
Soft drinks	Boissons sans alcool	Limonade
Mineral water	Eau minéral	Mineraalwater
Starter	Hors d'œuvre	Entrée
Main course	Plat principal	Hoofdgerecht
Dessert	Dessert	Nagerecht
Dish of the day	Plat du jour	Dagschotel
It tastes good	C'est très bon	Het smaakt lekker
Fish	Poisson	Vis
Meat	Viande	Vlees
Snails	Escargots	Slakken
Leg	Gigot	Bout
Rare	Saignant	Rood
Medium	A point	Half doorbakken
Well done	Bien cuit	Gaar
Vegetables	Légumes	Groenten
Belgian endive/ chicory	Endive	Witloof
Mushroom	Champignon	Champignon
Apple	Pomme	Appel
Pear	Poir	Peer
Cheese	Fromage	Kaas
Cake	Gâteau	Taart
Cheesecake	Tarte au fromage	Kaastaart
Whipped cream	Crème Chantilly	Slagroom
Ice cream	Glace	IJs
Waffle	Gaufre	Wafel
Could I have the bill please?	L'addition, s'il vous plaît	De rekening, alstublieft

Photo **Credits**